D1583925

MERSEYSIDE

THE INDIAN SUMMER

Volume 1

1 3 St

- 7 DEC 2

0 4 JAN 20

2 6

3 JUL 2012

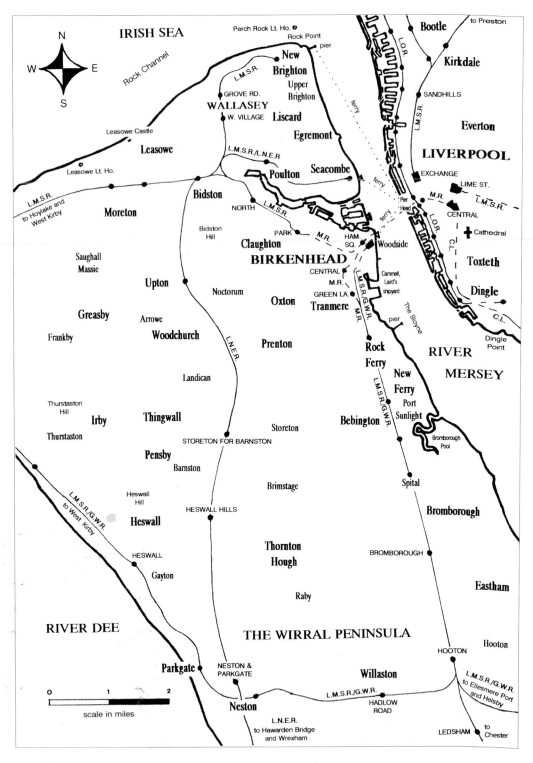

Map showing most of the places mentioned in the text of the two volumes, including the docks, piers, landing stages, railways and passenger stations. Broken lines are railway tunnels. Not shown are freight-only lines to the docks and industrial sites, or Liverpool Riverside station, which was just north of Pier Head, between Prince's Dock and the landing stage.

MERSEYSIDE

THE INDIAN SUMMER

Volume 1
Return to Woodside

Birkenhead • The Docks • The Ferries

CEDRIC GREENWOOD

ST. HELENS
COMMUNITY
LIBRARIES

ACC. No.
A11

CLASS No.
942.75

·THE HERITAGE OF BRITAIN·
from
The NOSTALGIA Collection

© Cedric Greenwood 2007

All rights reserved. No part of this publication may be reproduced, stored in a retrieval system or transmitted, in any form or by any means, electronic, mechanical, photocopying, recording or otherwise, without prior permission in writing from Silver Link Publishing Ltd.

First published in 2007

British Library Cataloguing in Publication Data

A catalogue record for this book is available from the British Library.

ISBN 978 1 85794 272 9

Silver Link Publishing Ltd
The Trundle
Ringstead Road
Great Addington
Kettering
Northants NN14 4BW

Tel/Fax: 01536 330588
email: sales@nostalgiacollection.com
Website: www.nostalgiacollection.com

Printed and bound in Great Britain

All photographs and drawings are by the author unless otherwise credited.

Front cover picture The busy bus and railway terminus at Birkenhead Woodside in 1961. Steam ferries plied from here across the Mersey to Liverpool every 10 or 15 minutes. Woodside was the focal point of life on the Cheshire bank, and the springboard to our adventures on Merseyside in the mid-20th century.
Back cover picture The last steam ferry on the Mersey, *Wallasey* (1927-63), photographed in 1961. *Both Cedric Greenwood*

CONTENTS

Left **HAMILTON SQUARE AND TOWN HALL, BIRKENHEAD**, see here in 1961, is where the prosaic streets of workaday Birkenhead meet in one of the most dignified Georgian squares in Britain, reminiscent of Edinburgh's Georgian New Town. The shipbuilder and land-owner William Laird, from Greenock, engaged a fellow Scotsman, one of Edinburgh New Town's surveyors and architects, Gillespie Graham, to lay out the classical grid of streets of the new town bounded by Chester Street, Conway Street, Cleveland Street and Duke Street, and to design the terraced houses of Hamilton Square in the town centre. The concept of Laird, Graham and the Birkenhead Improvement Commissioners was to build the whole of Birkenhead in the late-Georgian, or Regency, style of Hamilton Square, but only a few isolated classical terraces were built before the needs of industry and cheap housing altered the face of the town from 1847. It took 100 years to complete the Hamilton Square we see in this picture. The stone-faced terraced blocks of houses were built piecemeal from 1826 to 1846, the Town Hall (centre) in 1883-87, the clock tower in 1901, the Eleanor Cross (left) in the centre of the gardens in 1905 as a monument to Queen Victoria, and the cenotaph opposite the Town Hall in 1925. The Town Hall, with its Corinthian portico on the front and Sessions House at the back, fills the block between Mortimer Street (left) and Brandon Street (right), and the Sessions House fronts on to Chester Street. All the buildings in the square are faced in 'white' sandstone from Storeton Quarry, which turned black in 120 years of Merseyside smoke. A start on stone cleaning at the corner of Mortimer Street revealed the natural, pale grey-pink colour of the stone. Hamilton Square covers 6 acres in the centre of Birkenhead, and is one of the largest squares in Britain. The gardens were originally the private gardens of the houses around the square until they were acquired by the Corporation in 1903 and laid out as public gardens in their present form. The open aspect of the gardens preserves the intimate quadrangle concept of Georgian social town planning, while most other squares in London, Bath and Edinburgh are now hidden by trees that have grown up in the middle.

ACKNOWLEDGEMENTS

My thanks go to Steve Howe of The Black & White Picture Place, Hoole, Chester, and to Glynn Parry of Bromborough for their care in coaxing the best out of my box camera photographs of 1950-61. The pictures I took from 1961 onward are copied direct from my transparencies.

I have supplemented my own photographs with selected picture postcards I bought on Merseyside in the 1950s. Many of these pictures were published by Valentine & Sons of Dundee and I thank St Andrews University Library, which holds the major archive of Valentine's monochrome topographical views, for permission to reproduce the Valentine's postcards in this book and for providing me with the dates. I also thank Judges Postcards Ltd of Hastings and the Salmon Picture Library at Sevenoaks for permission to use the copyright on their picture postcards. Many of the other postcard publishers are now extinct and I cannot trace any copyright holders and many picture postcards reproduced here are anonymous. The Williamson Art Gallery & Museum at Birkenhead provided the prints of William Herdman's paintings of Tranmere in 1868 and Woodside Ferry in 1814 and the aerial photograph of Birkenhead docks, and Birkenhead Library supplied an anonymous engraving of Birkenhead's first horse-tram on Argyle Street. Pages from the Birkenhead and Liverpool guide books of 1950-51 are reproduced by permission of Wirral Borough Council and Liverpool City Council. All the postcards and guide books I have used here are from my own collection.

In writing the text I have often referred to the following local residents, who have cheerfully shared their specialist knowledge: the late Jack Barlow of West Kirby; Jack Gahan of Fairfield, Liverpool; Joyce Hockey of New Brighton; Bruce Maund of Oxton; Glynn Parry of Bromborough; Edgar Richards of Bebington; John Ryan of Bromborough; Angus Tilston of Bebington; Tom Turner of Upper Brighton; and Robbie Warburton of Rock Ferry (now of Eastham). I am indebted to the reference library staff of the Birkenhead Central Library for patiently plying me with old street directories and maps and posting me photocopies of entries in the directories I had overlooked. I am also indebted to the courtesy of staff of Norwich reference library, the National Railway Museum at York, Unilever Archives at Port Sunlight, the *Liverpool Daily Post & Echo* library and the Office for National Statistics at Newport (Mon). I should also single out the following officers who have supplied me with literature or given their time to answer my questions: Brian Forster (operations manager) of Mersey Wharf, Bromborough; John Coleman (president) of Birkenhead District Scout Council; Philip Bastow (honorary secretary and historian) of the Royal Mersey Yacht Club; David Jones (commodore) of Tranmere Sailing Club; Dr Graham Patience (managing director) of Stone Manganese Marine Ltd; the late R. S. Cowan (general manager) of Birkenhead Corporation Ferries (1937 to 1955); Captain Dennis Titherington (now retired marine operations manager) and Peter Hester (present operations manager) of Mersey Ferries; Joan Roberts (marketing and publicity officer) of Friends of the Ferries Across the Mersey; and Jo-Anne Colby of Canadian Pacific Railway Archives, Montreal.

PROLOGUE: MY MERSEYSIDE

It was little more than 50 years ago, but the Mersey scene I first beheld from the top deck of a Birkenhead ferry crossing the river to Liverpool was a world apart from the run-down, sanitised, twilight towns on the Mersey estuary today. Crossing the docks on the top deck of a Birkenhead bus to Wallasey by night was sheer magic to this wide-eyed Southern boy at the age of 11. I think it takes the eye of a stranger to appreciate the special character of a place and see things that local people take for granted. I count myself lucky to have lived at Wallasey in the years 1949 to 1952, when the port of Liverpool and the seaside resort of New Brighton were thriving in a post-war peak of prosperity. After two World Wars and an inter-war trade recession, the late 1940s and early 1950s was a period of almost full employment.* Industry, commerce, transport, entertainment and almost all spheres of British life were at a new zenith. Trade in the port of Liverpool was booming as never before.

The three years I lived there were the happiest and most memorable years of my life because of the location and the period. I was at the impressionable age of 11 to 14 and Merseyside at the beginning of the 1950s was a very interesting place for a boy to grow up in. All was grist to my mill: the shipping in the river and docks, a fishing fleet of sailing boats moored off New Brighton, the quaint steam engines that ambled through dockland streets with long goods trains, horse-drawn wagons and steam lorries at the great, dusty warehouses, and the pioneer electric trains on the Liverpool Overhead Railway and the Mersey (underground) Railway. Large, arched-roofed railway terminals echoed to hissing steam and shrieking whistles. The ubiquitous Liverpool tramcars glided and hummed eerily through the labyrinth of one-way slum streets and along the high-speed grass-track reservations of the outer suburbs. The great steam ferries dating from the 1920s and '30s stole silently across a millpond river by night or rolled heavily in the storms that blew in from the Irish Sea.

In those post-war years, when cars were scarce, the buses and trams were part of our everyday life and a key element of the street scene; their shapes and colours part of the local identity. The street scene was enlivened by the kaleidoscope of buses: Crosville and Liverpool grass green, Birkenhead mid-blue, Wallasey primrose, Ribble crimson, St Helens scarlet and cream, and Lancashire United vermilion and light grey. Half the cars, lorries and buses and all the trams on our streets dated from the 1930s. All vehicles were British and had distinctive identities. Our ships, railways, buses and trams showed innate good sense of practical and aesthetic design and tasteful paint schemes. Reliability and efficiency were high in public services, and we were proud of our Corporation buses and ferries.

Life on Merseyside was set against a background of masts, derricks, cranes and satanic, smoking mills of dockland on both sides of the river, the wooded ridge with its windmill above the rooftops of Birkenhead, the wide, empty, tree-lined streets of Wallasey, the succession of ocean-going liners and freighters parading past the noble and impressive architecture of Liverpool city centre, the view across Liverpool Bay, with its wide, sandy shores and dunes, and the convoys of ships to and from all parts of the world, seen against the dramatic backdrop of the Welsh mountains on our western horizon. Merseyside was grey, grim and grimy, but it was a busy working scene, charged with character, atmosphere and interest. It was fun to be there and it was a very different place from what is left of it today. It was so much a world apart from the ordinary urban and rural environment in Britain that those who never saw it could not imagine what it was like. No other great river so imposed itself on its urban environment and the everyday lives of its people as the mighty Mersey and its shipping, docks and ferries, and associated

* The unemployment rate nationally and in the North West region was 1.5 per cent in 1950, compared with 5.5 and 5.3 per cent respectively in June 2006. The rate for Merseyside, usually higher than the national and regional figures, dropped from 5.3 per cent in June 1948 to 2.6 per cent in June 1951, when the national figure was 1 per cent, an all-time low.

industries and commerce. No other great port was so close to the sea.

I had lived at Hove and Oxford before Dad's work in the Post Office Telephones moved to Liverpool and we settled in Wallasey. I was not unprepared for what I saw. Oxford had slums that were meaner than anything I saw on Merseyside. I was fascinated by the Black Country scene from the train on the way to Birkenhead. And Liverpool reminded me of Harry Lime's Vienna, which we had seen at the cinema in 1949. I saw a certain quaintness in scenes from the industrial 19th century and Victorian Gothic buildings when they were generally disregarded as ugly, but in this I was 30 years ahead of my time. By the 1980s we began to lament the losses of the 1960s and to cherish and preserve our remaining industrial and Victorian heritage.

Obviously Merseyside made a great impression on me because I lived there for no more than 12 months of the three years that it was my home. I carried on schooling at Oxford and travelled home by train only at half-term and the end of term. I can still recite the names of all 84 stations and halts in those 165½ miles from Oxford General to Birkenhead Woodside, most of which have since disappeared. I used to admire a poster on the wooden station buildings on the down platform at Oxford, a powerfully atmospheric and very evocative painting of the smoky Mersey from Woodside. That picture would materialise at the end of my journey.

I took an interest in local history and the Mersey ferries when I lived at Wallasey, and I can date that interest to two booklets of 1949 – *Wallasey Old And New* and *The History Of Wallasey's Famous Ferry Services* – and to 1952, when the general manager of Birkenhead Corporation Ferries lent me his sole copy of the history and annals of the six ferries from Woodside to New Ferry from 1284 to 1938, and I copied it laboriously by hand into a school exercise-book. I became fascinated by 18th- and early 19th-century maps and pictures of the topography of Wallasey and Birkenhead and the ferry landing places. From that has stemmed my interest in the local history of everywhere I have lived, but I find the local history and old picture postcards of Merseyside more interesting than anywhere else.

Dad's career found me living in Hove, Oxford, Wallasey and Herne Bay, and my career took me on to Kendal, Southport, Campbeltown, Chester and north Norfolk – all nice places, but the truth is that I enjoyed living in Wallasey most of all, at that period. I probably would not choose to live in Wallasey now because I am too aware of what has been lost, but in its northern parts it is still the most pleasant residential town I know. Back in the 1950s it had an interesting port and a pleasant rural hinterland on its doorstep.

I began taking these photographs of Merseyside in 1950, when I was 12 years old, but most of them were taken after we left. Dad's work moved to Canterbury in 1952 and we lived at Herne Bay. Kent was pleasant and interesting enough but I missed Merseyside; to me it had much more atmosphere and interest. I consoled myself by strolling around the London riverside wharves and warehouses from Southwark to Limehouse, then still busy with ships and cargoes.

In those days there was a daily through train from Margate to Birkenhead via Guildford and Oxford. It used to thrill me to see the name Birkenhead on the carriage route boards as it rolled across St Dunstan's Street, Canterbury, at 10.03am. Birkenhead Woodside was the ultimate terminus, the 'ultima Thule', of the modest travel aspirations of this boy with his bicycle and box camera. That combined terminus of railway, ferry and buses on the headland by the Mersey was the springboard to the whole Merseyside adventure.

When I was 16 I boarded that train at Canterbury West and spent two weeks on Merseyside with my bicycle and box camera with the specific intention of photographing the streets, docks and ferries. I also recorded some of the country lanes of Wirral. Most of the photographs in this book were taken then, between 21 August and 4 September 1954, and they represent quite a large expenditure in eight-picture roll films for a schoolboy saving his modest pocket money of that period. I wanted to show people what a place of character it was. And now I am. I am glad I took these photographs when I did.

Dad had graduated to a glass-plate camera and passed down his 1925-vintage Kodak No 2 Brownie 120 box camera to me. These photographs were taken with a fixed shutter speed of 1/25th of a second, using three apertures; moreover, as you had to hold the camera on your tummy, the viewfinder, only 9mm by 12mm, was 1 foot away from your eyes. You could hardly see what you had in the picture frame.

From 1957 onwards I returned to Merseyside just for a few days every year. It was an essential part of my annual holiday itinerary and on those visits I took several more of the photographs that appear here: black and white box camera pictures till 1961, then colour transparencies with a Braun Paxette 35mm camera until the 1970s. By that time most of my Merseyside had been demolished or changed so radically that there was nothing left to photograph. I have used some post-1960 transparencies here for a more complete record of the townscape, but only those scenes that show the unadulterated fabric of the 1950s. I have also used some of Dad's photographs (those by the late George Greenwood) and picture postcards I bought there in the 1950s to illustrate some key features of the townscape not covered in my own photographs.

In these pictures we are looking at Merseyside in its element, its post-war heyday, the Indian summer of the old civilisation of the Industrial Age before the decline set in – the time when we called our homeland Britain, not the anonymous UK – but it is essentially a view of Merseyside from the Cheshire bank. When I say Merseyside I mean the towns on the banks of the estuary, as it was understood in the period under review, not the short-lived administrative county of Merseyside that existed from 1974 to 1986 or the area served by the residual boroughs and combined public services.

This was the twilight of what we might also call the Coal Age and the Steam Age, of horse haulage, canal freight, city tramways and ocean liners. Great Britain was still the workshop of the world and had the finest shipyards and the largest merchant fleet in the world. The post-war period was the heyday of the port of Liverpool in terms of imports, exports and passengers. It was not till 1957 that more people began to travel overseas by air than by sea, and we still used propellers for both. The first jet airliner entered service in 1958.

As a boy growing up in the 1950s I could be forgiven for thinking that nothing would change, but of course change is an inevitable part of evolution. Everything is undergoing metamorphosis all the time and the changing face of Merseyside is part of that process. Change was rapid in the 19th century, but then Britain was in the ascendancy and led the world in the peak 100 years of the Industrial Age. Change was rapid and radical in the second half of the 20th century too, but this time Britain was in decline.

I felt at the time – even then, at the age of 17 – that 1955 was the watershed year when Britain had achieved its optimum development and civilisation began to regress, slowly and almost imperceptibly at first. The decline was brought about by economic and social change. The year 1955 was the year of introduction of commercial television with advertisements, which brought an end to the golden age of radio. It was the year that gave birth to the modernisation programme for British Railways, which spelled the end of steam and the decimation of a true railway network that could carry goods from and to almost any point in Britain. It was the year that also gave birth to the road programme for a national network of motorways, which generated more traffic. The two programmes combined to put more and bigger lorries on our roads, streets and lanes.

The second half of the decade saw the first signs of the times to come: the run-down of coal mines, steelworks, shipyards and heavy engineering, the demise of public transport and cinemas, traffic jams in towns, double yellow lines, parking meters, supermarkets, multi-storey flats, G-plan furniture, rock 'n' roll, race riots and football hooliganism. The end of our steam and gaslight era was nigh.

The year 1956 saw the closure of the Liverpool Overhead Railway and the end of passenger trains on the charming rural branch line from Hooton to West Kirby. In the same year those who sailed on the day excursion to Llandudno lost the thrill of a ride on an open-top tram over the hills from Llandudno to Colwyn Bay. In 1957 Liverpool's great tramway system, which had been in demise since 1948, came to an end with the closure of the last two lines, to Bowring Park and Page Moss. Over the period 1957 to 1959 Liverpool lost a landmark as the girders of the Overhead Railway came down, and the city seemed strangely deserted without the Overhead and the trams.

THE DECLINE

The cold wind of change blew through Merseyside in the 1960s. Passenger figures were in sharp decline on the ferries and the buses, while motor cars queued for the Mersey Tunnel. This was a period of economy and austerity and we were ruled by Philistines, who tore down the Doric arch and Great Hall at Euston, and even the St Pancras station hotel was under threat. Hitler bombed hell out of Merseyside, but our modernisers and developers devastated the place and created more wasteland in the second half of the 20th century than Hitler ever did. On both sides of the Mersey the friendly old townscapes gave way to a new, austere environment with no sense of townscape at all. Victorian brick and stone buildings were pulled down to make way for grim blocks of offices and flats in concrete and coloured glass, supermarkets with blank frontages and concrete viaducts called flyovers, while the old streets were disfigured with gantry signs for the conquering motor car. Familiar main streets were blocked up and one-way traffic schemes led drivers on quite unnecessary, circuitous mystery tours of mutilated and unrecognisable tracts of our own towns. Merely a comparison of street maps of the 1950s and today shows how radically the place has changed.

When I revisited Merseyside from Kendal in 1967 to make a documentary audiotape programme, My Merseyside, I found that I had left it too late: my Merseyside no longer existed. Trains stopped running from Paddington to Woodside in March 1967; I made the pilgrimage from Paddington on the last day. Rock Ferry Pier and the hulks of the shipbreakers' yard on the Tranmere shore, where I had spent many happy hours as a boy, had been removed and replaced by a great new ocean oil terminal. All the steam ferries had gone and been replaced by diesel vessels. The routine drama of the Seacombe Ferry bus ritual had ceased and the buses stood casually about Victoria Place with no formation, no discipline and no mass exodus.

Liverpool Pier Head was cluttered with a range of 1960s buildings like a stack of orange boxes atop the river wall, a disgrace to the Liver, Cunard and Dock Buildings and blocking the view of the river. The slowly moving sea of green on Pier Head was now a milling mass of diesel buses instead of electric trams. (The bus terminus and its kiosks, cafe and offices have now gone.) There were no more wooden electric trains rumbling overhead to Dingle or underground to Birkenhead, no horse wagons or steam lorries or steam trains still working in dockland, no children playing traditional street games on chalked pavements. There was nothing for me to record at all.

The Liverpool dock road, bereft of the Overhead Railway alongside and the arcaded warehouses along the middle, was now a wide, windy gash across the townscape and a six-lane race-track for cars and diesel lorries that cut off the Pier Head from the rest of the city. Everywhere there was an air of desolation with extensive clearance sites and many empty, condemned and boarded-up buildings. Liverpool called itself the 'City of Change and Challenge', but I could not help being reminded of the words of the hymn: '...change and decay in all around I see...'.

In November 1967 Woodside station closed. What was then the only listed station on Merseyside was flattened for a car park. The great train shed was a key feature of the townscape and its loss left the ferry approach wide open. Birkenhead was beheaded, then its heart was cut out as what was left of the town centre was laid waste for new approach roads to the Mersey Tunnel. The nasty 1960s produced a nine-storey municipal office block of buff concrete and dark glass in one corner of Hamilton Square and a grim wall of 11-storey flats in the slum clearance area. Almost all the work our forefathers had done to create Birkenhead in the period 1840 to 1880 was undone in the 1960s and '70s.

The closure of Woodside station was followed by the closure of Liverpool Riverside station in 1971, Liverpool Central in 1972 and Liverpool Exchange in 1977. Riverside closed as most of the passenger liners had left Liverpool for Southampton. While passenger shipping had declined, cargoes handled in the docks on both sides of the river had continued to rise to a peak (in terms of weight) of 29 million tons in 1969, but then rapidly dwindled to 9 million tons by 1984, when most of dockland lay derelict on both sides of the river.

Restrictive working practices and strikes in the

docks in the 1960s and '70s led to a loss of confidence by shippers, who switched their trade to the container port of Felixstowe, nearer Europe. Cheaper imports led to the decline of heavy industries such as coal, steel and shipbuilding, helped by changes in patterns of supply and demand, trade and traffic. At the same time the transition from the engineering age to the electronic age combined to run down all the great industrial areas of Britain and their ports. This drained the lifeblood from Birkenhead and Liverpool with its ship-related industries and commerce, and the great mills and warehouses became silent and empty. When New Brighton Ferry closed in 1971 and the last liner left Liverpool in 1972, we knew that this was the end of the real Merseyside.

The evolutionary changes seen since the 1950s have taken place in the context of the breakdown of the society and civilisation and the disintegration of the infrastructure and balance of trade that had been built up over the previous 100 years. The change in society has produced a general indiscipline and indifference reflected in the scruffy, ugly, tawdry appearance of our built environment, especially in the former industrial areas. We now have clean air zones and advances in technology and medical science, but these have been offset by the deterioration of the urban environment and quality of life.

In the last 35 years we have inflicted on ourselves not only the destruction of our environment in the name of modernisation but also decimalisation of our currency, metrication of our weights and measures, re-organisation of our local government, privatisation of our national utilities, municipal services, railways and buses, and the deregulation of those services. This has had a destabilising effect on our society. You would think that we could have got things right at some time after all these years, but our masters seem to be fatefully drawn into a vortex of periodic re-organisation for its own sake.

Inflation was rampant in the second half of the century. Nowhere in my text have I tried to equate the pounds, shillings and pence (£ s d) in 1950 with today's decimal currency. The nominal comparisons often given in books are only good for Decimalisation Day in 1971, when 1 shilling (1s)

became 5 new pence (5p), and 1 new penny equalled 2.4 denarii or old pence. (Pre-decimalisation there were 20 shillings or 240 pence in the pound.) Instead, values are related to the weekly wage, which in 1950 averaged £7 5s 10d (gross) for men. With inflation, £1 in 1950 was worth much more than £1 in 1971, which was, in turn, worth far more than £1 today, and 1 shilling was worth much more than 5p, so comparisons based on the 1971 conversion are worthless. The Woodside ferry toll to Liverpool (single) in 1949-55 was 2½d for adults and 1d for children. At the oft-quoted 1971 conversion rate these tolls would equate to slightly less than 1p and ½p respectively. In 2006 the ferry tolls were £1.35 for adults and £1.05 for children (single), which shows that inflation has multiplied the adult toll 130 times and the child toll 252 times in the 50 years since 1955. The 1d toll last paid by children in 1955 had remained unchanged since 1922.

TWILIGHT TOWNS

I am a Merseyside exile. I cannot go back there because Merseyside does not exist any more. It is still there geographically in terms of towns alongside the river, but the life has gone out of it, the soul is dead, it has lost its identity.

While in the 1950s it was always a thrill for me to revisit Merseyside, through the 1960s, '70s and '80s I looked forward to it less and less. In 1973 I bought a 1951 Wallasey Corporation bus when it was retired from service. It was one of the last of the line of 130 buses of a Wallasey standard design dating from 1937 and I restored it as an ambassador for Wallasey. I took it out for Sunday constitutionals and annual club excursions over extinct Wallasey bus routes of the 1950s. If I stopped in the street for 5 minutes the cameras came out of the houses and the nostalgia among ordinary people over a certain age surprised and gratified me. At first it was just like old times, but our journeys into nostalgia could not hold the clock back. Year by year the setting changed, particularly on the joint routes in Birkenhead. Over the years of these excursions we saw the deterioration of the roads, the run-down of the shopping centres and the disfigurement of the townscape, and found our operations gradually circumscribed by lowering trees, blocked streets and one-way traffic systems. By the year 2000 we could follow only three of the original 20 Wallasey bus routes (the 12, 17 and 18) both ways without diversions. I was very attached to my bus for 30 years. I did not change, the bus did not change, but the outside world changed. I drove my last excursion in 2003; I could face it no longer, and I was content to transfer ownership of the bus to the borough transport museum in Birkenhead, where it was already stabled.

Now I no longer want to visit Merseyside. The experience is too unpleasant. I have a love-hate relationship with the place. I love what it was and the vestiges of the old, such as can still be found in Port Sunlight, Oxton, Claughton, Upper Brighton, Wallasey and parts of rural Wirral, but I hate the scruffy, semi-derelict shopping, industrial and resort areas and being fenced in by so many miles of suburbia and motorways. The face of Merseyside has changed 50 per cent in the last 50 years – more in some places than others – and the character and atmosphere have changed 100 per cent. The people have changed. Even the Merseyside accents have changed in the new generations.

When I went back to Merseyside to pinpoint the locations of some of the pictures of Birkenhead, almost everywhere I went I met with blank spaces, stark concrete walls, security fencing, weeds, litter, graffiti and parked cars. Roads have been blocked up and streets have disappeared. Roads of houses and shops for people have become dual carriageways of 'landscaping' through no-man's-land unfit for human existence. Fifty years ago the entire scene was busy with people, but relatively few people live and work there now. Redevelopment has not kept pace with demolition and vast tracts of Birkenhead and Liverpool are unrecognisable urban deserts. New supermarkets turn their blank facades to the street frontage and the old butchers', bakers', grocers' and greengrocers' shops lie empty or are converted to off-licence drink stores, fast food take-aways or betting shops. Those banks, hotels and warehouses that are not derelict have been converted to bars, restaurants, night clubs and flats, and the streets are littered with fast food wrappings and shoals of broken glass. Jack Gahan, author of five books about Merseyside railways and dockland, said to me: 'I used to love every square yard of Liverpool. Now I hate it.'

I do not advise anyone to go and look at these scenes today, because all they will find is ugliness or wilderness. Neither would I depress my readers by showing pictures of the same scenes today in a 'then and now' exercise; that would be a waste of space. People who live there know what it is like and those who are not familiar with Merseyside would probably not wish to know. My purpose here is to reconstruct Merseyside of the 1950s in words and pictures, not to destroy it in the next breath. That is why I have not outlined any scene changes since 1960 in the captions, except to follow the fortunes of certain individual institutions such as cinemas, piers and ferry steamers. While I have used the present tense in the captions to describe what is happening in the pictures, I have had to use past and present tenses in my general narrative to distinguish between what is extinct and what is extant.

I am writing the content of what would normally be the epilogue (or perhaps I should say epitaph) here in the prologue rather than at the end of the book so that the reader can appreciate how much change has taken place in only 50 years, but is left at the end with an impression of the way most of us would prefer to remember it. Although I have deliberately not included any comparison views of the present day, I have, conversely, included some 'flashback' views of selected locations – Rock Ferry, Tranmere, Birkenhead, Woodside Ferry, New Brighton and Liverpool Landing Stage – from 1814 to 1924 in a 'then and before' exercise. They show how relatively little change there was in the previous 100 years compared with the last 50 years and, in most cases, how much better the place looked in the older pictures. It is a story in pictures of steady decline. For the record, and for readers who are not familiar with Merseyside today, I feel I should summarise the main changes that have taken place since these photographs were taken.

There is now no main-line railway to Birkenhead. The route from Paddington is broken into four sections, and the four-track approach to Birkenhead has narrowed to two tracks that carry no freight. Suburban electric trains run through a lineside wilderness and bleak stations with 'corporate' yellow paintwork and go underground from Rock Ferry.

The paradise of Port Sunlight, a Grade II listed conservation area, is now traversed by through traffic on two routes between Bebington and New Ferry. This is the price we paid to block up part of Bebington Road, New Ferry, as a shopping 'precinct' with the usual street clutter.

The A41 Rock Ferry by-pass scythes through the Victorian residential oasis of Rock Park, cutting off the town centre from its riverfront. The main street has lost its shops, which have been replaced by 'landscaped' open spaces that reach right up to the signals in the town centre, and by modern factory sheds that turn their backs on the street frontage. Tranmere oil terminal has impinged on the pier and the riverfront is a scene of utter dereliction. How can we allow our environment to degenerate to this when all property is owned by somebody, and with central and local agencies for the environment?

Cammell, Laird's shipyard has closed and been converted to an industrial estate with residual ship repairs by A&P in the old fitting-out basin. Almost the whole town centre of Birkenhead has been devastated by demolition and dereliction and is lost in a maze of modern shopping 'precincts'. A flyover cuts across the pleasant square at the junction of Argyle Street and Borough Road, but the one on Conway Street has been taken down, as have all the grim skyscrapers of the 1960s, so those blots on the townscape proved to be unnecessary. The town centre is hardly recognisable except for the restored Georgian and post-Georgian terraces of Hamilton Square and some surrounding streets.

The broad square of Woodside ferry approach is cluttered with poles and a conspicuous new bus station that is empty most of the time. It has lost its backdrop of the grand railway terminus but has regained a tram terminus – if only of a line from the borough transport museum. The much-altered hotel is only partly used as a bar and restaurant, and the emasculated ferry tollhouse, with its shortened colonnade, is still the ferry entrance and now also a restaurant and tourist information centre. This focal point of the town should be retained and developed as a fine square with appropriate buildings matching Hamilton Street,

not covered with building blocks as shown in the Woodside master plan.

I still get a thrill as I cycle down the slope of Chester Street or Hamilton Street to the ferry with the view across the tearing tideway to Liverpool Pier Head and the sandstone Cathedral, when I breathe the salty air and see the ferry swinging into the stage. But the spell is broken as I stand on the river wall and see that the ferry is the only vessel on the river, the sanitised Liver Building no longer boldly dominates the Mersey scene and the Pier Head trinity is dwarfed by an ever-changing skyline of alien high-rise blocks of universal architecture under an equally uncharacteristic Mediterranean blue sky.

The ferry survives as the preferable alternative to the road or railway tunnel to Liverpool, but the tolls have gone up by some incalculable percentage since 1955 and one vessel now substitutes for four on the Woodside and Seacombe passages on a half-hourly triangular service in the peak period only, and an hourly cruise up and down the river in the off-peak. Passenger trips dropped from 27 million on the Woodside and Seacombe services in 1949-50 to 665,000 on the combined ferry service and river cruise in 2005-6. The ferries still cruise up the Ship Canal to Salford in the summer, but the dance cruises, once twice-daily, are now only occasional evening river cruises, and there are no more trips out to sea.

The combined ferry fleet has reduced from 11 vessels in 1950 to three vessels today. Gone are the stately, stealthy steamers with tall funnels, brown, wooden saloons and spacious promenade decks. Today we have noisy, vibrating diesels, slightly smaller than the steamers, with stumpy funnels, white, steel deckhouses, cluttered promenade decks and bulky bridges that mask the funnels from the bow view. Although recently refitted and remodelled, they date from 1960-62 and are still of traditional Mersey ferry design, shipshape and rugged, and not the floating glasshouses of London River.

All three landing stages have been replaced and are smaller. The glassy new Woodside stage and bridge of 1985 echo the barrel-roofs of the old ferry landing and the place retains some of the old stage furniture to complement the listed tollhouse. The half-mile Liverpool landing stage was 100 years old when it was replaced in 1975 by a short, three-berth, concrete-reinforced steel stage for Mersey ferries and Manx ships. This austere structure with a tent-like shelter and garish decor was the new entrance to Liverpool. The new stage was prone to sinking so the ferries are (in 2006) using a temporary pontoon from Holland while a new two-berth stage is built. With some foresight the architect of Seacombe stage (1999) designed it to look like a space station with its superstructure on a tubular steel A-frame; in 2005 Spaceport, with an observatory and planetarium, opened in the former two-storey garage for cars of ferry patrons behind the bus-loading colonnade.

The planned grid of streets west of Woodside has, for the second time around, been developed piecemeal without a master building plan. New houses with front and back gardens and new factories offer better living and working conditions but they do not form a coherent townscape. Many of the houses turn their backs to the street and large tracts of open space have not been redeveloped.

Dockland, once filled with ships, warehouses and railway yards, is another desert of empty open spaces of water, wasteland and scrap heaps – scrap metal now being one of our staple exports. Morpeth Branch Dock, Wallasey Dock, Bidston Dock and two of the dry docks on the West Float have been filled in. The Mersey Docks & Harbour Company has invested in fully mechanised handling of bulk cargoes and a duty-free transhipment zone, so the docks are still partly used, mainly for the import of oil, steel and timber, and mothballed ships, but there is very little sign of activity. Ship repairs and conversions are still done in the remaining dry dock on the West Float. New industrial estates are growing in dockland but again they do not seem to be planned to form a townscape.

Along the Mersey bank, Wallasey (Dock) Landing Stage has been replaced by the terminus of a vehicular ferry to Dublin and Belfast, and oil-tankers still berth at Tranmere. Bromborough Pool and Bromborough Dock, where Unilever imported oils for soap and margarine, have been filled in and the residual Mersey Wharf is operated by the Victoria Group, together with docks at Boston, Seaham, Sharpness and Plymouth. It imports granite, steel, timber and bulk raw materials, and exports aluminium and fertiliser.

The main scene changes in Wallasey, Liverpool and the Wirral hinterland, including Ellesmere Port, are summarised in Volume 2. Mersey shipping has seen a revival of trade in Liverpool's north docks and the Manchester Ship Canal, together with the return of ocean liners on cruises.

TOURISM

We even invite tourists to Merseyside today and there are many places of interest to see – if you pick your way through the bleak and scruffy austerity in between. Why did we not bring tourists to Merseyside in the 1950s, when the whole scene was much more interesting? I think the tourists have come too late; we have locked the door after the horse has bolted. Passengers on the river cruise and visitors to Liverpool Maritime Museum and the Birkenhead Heritage Trail are told about the glories of our industrial past. If the tourists had come in 1950 they could have seen it for themselves.

Even as late as 1984, when I made a cine film of Birkenhead Ferry with scenes ashore, I recorded three subjects that were killed off in the run-up to tourism. The Pier Hotel at Woodside was an unusual single-storey corner tavern with curvaceous Art Nouveau glazing bars, frosted designs in the window panes and the name picked out in cut glass in the frosted glazing of the double doors. In the late 1980s the tavern was closed and gutted for 'refurbishment' in a conservation area and new offices were stacked on top, detracting from its singular appearance. The gutted tavern, with plain glass and single doors, and the new offices above remain empty, and the condition of the Pier Hotel is worse than ever; it has no potential for re-use with the forest of pillars supporting the two empty floors above. If these buildings remain empty after all this time, who will occupy the high-density, labyrinthine redevelopment envisaged in the Woodside master plan with its cubist blocks and skyscrapers?

My film also showed gas lamps still glowing along Shore Road and railway tracks in wood-block paving on E Bridge. These were the last working gas lamps in Wirral, and Shore Road was designated the main street of Birkenhead's heritage trail and tramway, linking Woodside Ferry and the Mersey Railway pumping station (with its beam engine) at one end with the preserved E Bridge and the original Egerton Dock at the other. Shore Road was also part of the route of Britain's first tramway. The gas lamps and dock railway tracks and all the industrial buildings bar the Cheshire Lines goods station were removed from Shore Road and the wood-block paving and railway tracks on E Bridge were replaced with asphalt.

Hong Kong tramcars were bought for the 'heritage' tramway. What was the tourist interest in riding a Hong Kong tramcar along a neutered Shore Road? Enthusiasts saved the situation by restoring old Birkenhead, Wallasey and Liverpool tramcars to working order for service, and the line now leads to an interesting municipal transport museum in a brick building in Lord Street, which looks like an old tram shed but had no transport history and had to be adapted.

When Woodside station closed in 1967, I mooted the idea of keeping the listed station as a Merseyside transport museum with steam trains meeting British Railways at Rock Ferry. The live steam element would have performed a useful connection for visitors. The cavernous train shed could also have housed the preserved Liverpool & Manchester locomotive *Lion* of 1838, the Mersey Railway locomotive *Cecil Raikes* of 1885, the Liverpool Overhead electric car of 1893 and the LMS Wirral and Southport electric stock of 1938-39 drawn up alongside the platforms, the preserved steam lorries, buses and other road vehicles along the cab road between platforms 1 and 2, and large and small static relics on the concourse. Photographs and archives could have been displayed in the Gothic-windowed offices, and the baronial booking hall could have been the depot for tramcars sallying forth along the route of Britain's first tramway from Woodside Ferry to Birkenhead Park. A preserved Mersey steam ferry could have been berthed at a southern extension of Woodside Landing Stage for cruises on the river, calling at the Albert Dock maritime museum. In the Philistine 1960s, when we were casting out everything old and antique furniture was 'going for a song', my suggestion fell on stony ground.

Today *Lion* is at Manchester and the other railway stock still languishes in store awaiting restoration and display. *Lion*, the LOR car and a Sentinel undertype steam tractor are belatedly destined for a Museum of Liverpool to be built at Mann Island and due to open in 2009. The LMS electric sets now belong to the National Railway Museum, York, and are at Kineton army depot in Warwickshire.

When crowds no longer trooped over the ferries, one of the listed ferry tollhouses at Woodside or Seacombe would have made a fine setting for a ferries museum, where all the models in glass cases, the old Woodside tollbooths and all the other relics, large and small, that survive in different places, could have been brought together to commemorate the most important factor in the making of Birkenhead and Wallasey and interest those taking the ferry cruise. Woodside tollhouse is now a café and visitor centre, Seacombe ferry buildings are home to a children's play area, an aquarium and a planetarium, and there is still no ferries museum or consolidated ferries collection on display.

If Merseyside were unchanged from the place it was in these photographs of the 1950s, it would be like one big museum or theme park and the tourist 'honeypot' of the world. It is precisely because of the decline and the uncongenial mess the modernisers have made of the place that I want to show people how much character, interest and atmosphere Merseyside had in relatively recent times. Today people might discover Wallasey as a pleasant place to live. If only they knew how much more pleasant it had been only 50 years ago. It is a great pity that its character was not preserved or its potential enhanced instead of being spoiled and neglected. When I revisited Merseyside annually over the last six years to make further references for this book, I could not help feeling that it was now being run by people who did not know or care anything about the place, past or present.

Probably older residents, who have lived through the insidious changes that have taken place piecemeal over the years, will not realise just how much change has gone on under their noses in that short period of history until they see these pictures. They will be less aware of change than somebody who revisits the place after an absence of, say, 40 years. I wish I had never returned to Merseyside after 1959 to see the place mutilated; I would prefer to remember it as it was in these pictures.

BACK TO THE 1950s

We are putting the calendar back to the year 1950 and looking at Birkenhead and Wallasey in happier, less hurried, more civilised times. Observe that the main streets are busy with people, not motor traffic, and the residential streets look wider because they are empty of parked cars. You will see no patchwork of tarmac, no yellow lines and very few white lines, no humps in the road, no caged or shuttered shop windows, no television aerials, no security cameras, very little litter, no graffiti, no footpaths spotted with chewing-gum, no cyclists on the footpaths – none of the features of the bleak, scruffy, modern, urban scene.

On the debit side there were no clean air zones either, the buildings were soot-black with coal smoke from houses, industry and shipping, there were unhealthy conditions in the docks and industries, and public health suffered from a general habit of smoking tobacco with no health warnings and from choking smogs (smoky fogs) that reduced visibility on the streets and the river to a few yards.

Observe also that everyone was properly dressed, even on the beaches, although gross wages averaged only £7 5s 10d for men and £4 0s 2½d for women, and there was no money to spare on anything but essentials. Men wore suits and ties and women wore printed cotton frocks or matching jackets and skirts with a hemline to mid-calf. Unless it was warm, dress was complete with overcoats or mackintoshes with the same hemline for men and women. Some men wore bowler hats, trilby hats or flat caps, and many women wore headscarves, but most men were hatless and clean shaven; hats and beards were not in fashion as they had been in the century before. Women did not wear trousers, except for some factory workers, farm hands and bus conductresses.

We see labourers wearing shabby old suits, flat caps and boots, and schoolboys smartly dressed in their school uniforms, often with cap, tie, short trousers and long, grey socks – and bear in mind that I took these photographs only in the school holidays; boys probably had little else to wear. The rebels of the period were Teddy Boys, and they were also smartly dressed in neo-Edwardian suits, but they are little in evidence here – there is one on Bedford Road bridge, Rock Ferry, and one on Brownlow Hill, Liverpool – and they did not drive motor cars.

People were generally rather lean. There is only one overweight person in the entire collection: he is waiting for a bus outside the Mersey Inn, Tranmere, smartly dressed in suit and tie. We were still living on wartime food rations till 1954, although tinned food was de-rationed in 1949 and sweets and chocolates in 1953. We could not afford to eat or drink too much. Sweets, chocolates and crisps were rare treats. And there were no plastic wrappings.

Many a woman in these pictures is complete with her own leather shopping-bag. If you did not have your own bag, the shopkeeper might supply a thick brown paper carrier-bag with string handles. Many goods were sold loose in paper bags, not pre-packed in plastic film or other impenetrable plastic packaging. One shopping bag or basket sufficed. In those days before supermarkets, mobile grocers, greengrocers, bakers, fishmongers and milkmen in motor vans or electric floats hawked their wares from house to house or made routine deliveries to your door.

This is a study in topography and townscape, not in social life and conditions, but the social environment is important in our appreciation of the physical environment and the two factors are related. This was the last decade before the public addiction to motoring and television changed our physical and social environment, our physique and social attitudes. It was the last decade of the old order before the permissive 1960s ushered in the decline of British civilisation. The biggest change I have seen in the past 50 years – more radical than the change in the environment – has been the degeneration of social behaviour. In dress and demeanour, 1950s man and woman would be as conspicuous today as today's man and woman would have been in the 1950s. There was a strong distinction between the genders.

A boy or girl could travel safely anywhere in the country. My parents gave me the freedom to ride

Leicester tramways at the age of 10. At the same age I made my first hitch-hiking journey, by lorry from scout camp in Hampshire to Oxford, just to save the bus fare (14s 6d) for pocket money. I travelled to and from school by train between Birkenhead and Oxford from the age of 11, and hitch-hiked all over Britain from 1953 till 1965. Hitch-hiking was then a safe and not uncommon form of travel, and usually quicker than travel by coach.

In these 1950s scenes, people were well-mannered, bright, brisk, breezy and cheerful, still imbued with the wartime 'chin-up' spirit of good humour, neighbourliness and mutual help, and the streets, stations, ferries and workplaces were as alive with the sound of men whistling as the country lanes were with the sound of birdsong.

Most people travelled sociably together by bus, tram, train, ferry, bicycle or on foot instead of using the public highway as a linear car park. We wasted no time waiting to cross the road in those days, and buses did not waste half their journey time at stops for drivers to issue the queue with tickets and change – the conductor did that while we were on our way.

Mothers stayed at home to look after the house and children; they did not have to go out to work, taking jobs from the men, to help pay the mortgage, and this contributed to full employment in the post-war heyday. The virtues of domesticity and motherhood were extolled in women's magazines of the period. Mother's role was important to the mental and emotional development of the children, who were brought up by their parents, schools and Sunday Schools with discipline and a strong sense of security and of right and wrong. The cane was still used at school and the noose was still the punishment for murder.

Colour came into the home in the 1950s, with bright new wallpapers, carpets, curtains and electric appliances such as refrigerators, food mixers and washing machines. The family had their meals around the table and spent their evenings and weekends reading, working on creative hobbies, listening to the radio or going to 'the pictures', by which they always meant the cinema, not the art gallery. In 1950 television was in its infancy, being broadcast on one BBC channel only a few hours each day to 300,000 viewers in the Home Counties and the Midlands (it came to Merseyside in the autumn of 1951). Radio closed down and the streetlights went off at midnight. Virtually the only life after midnight was in the docks and mills and steelworks. People worked hard in those days, but we never heard of stress at work, although it probably existed. The working week in office, factory and school ended at midday on Saturday, so Saturday night was the big night out at the bar, dance hall and cinema.

We did not take time off on New Year's Day, nor did we take weekdays off in lieu of Christmas Day and Boxing Day if they coincided with the weekend. Our fortnight's annual holidays were spent shoulder to shoulder in crowds on the promenades and beaches and in the holiday camps of Britain's seaside resorts, but during the 1950s some families ventured abroad on coach tours. Spanish seaside resorts were still unspoiled: no high-rise hotels, no marauding Britons.

The decade after the Second World War was the golden age of radio. Among the nation's favourite programmes were *Dick Barton – Special Agent*, *Down Your Way*, *Family Favourites*, *The Goon Show*, *Hancock's Half Hour*, *Have A Go*, *Ignorance Is Bliss*, *In Town Tonight*, *ITMA*, *Just William*, *Life With The Lyons*, *Much Binding In the Marsh*, *The Adventures of PC 49*, *Radio Forfeits*, *Stand Easy*, *Twenty Questions* and *Variety Bandbox*.

We remember with affection the voices of Bruce Belfrage, Freddy Grisewood, Wilfred Pickles, John Snagge and Wynford Vaughan-Thomas, and especially the comedians: 'Archie Andrews' (alias Peter Brough), Eric Barker, Michael Bentine, Dick Bentley, Max Bygraves, Charlie Chester, Sam Costa, Jimmy Edwards, Cyril Fletcher, Tony Hancock, Kenneth Horne, Frankie Howerd, Sid James, Hattie Jacques, Ben Lyons, Morecambe and Wise, Vic Oliver, Al Read, Derek Roy, Eric Sykes, Jack Warner, and Elsie and Doris Waters. Merseyside bred more comedians than anywhere else, and in this period we heard Arthur Askey, Deryck Guyler, Tommy Handley, Ted Ray and Robb Wilton. All these were the voices in our homes.

Another voice that was a household name was that of Dr Charles Hill, the Radio Doctor, who broadcast to the nation on the Home Service (now Radio 4) with advice on health and sickness in plain words with a quiet, dry, good humour. He became an MP in 1950 and later Postmaster General. Politics, like radio and films, was full of characters in those days, like Bessie Braddock, MP for Liverpool Exchange (1945-70); of course we also often heard the voice of the Prime Minister, Clement Attlee (1945-51), who nationalised utilities and gave us the National Health Service, Winston Churchill, our wartime leader, on his second term (1951-55), Sir Anthony Eden (1955-57) and Harold Macmillan (1957-63).

King George VI (1936-52) broadcast to the nation throughout the war. This shy but gregarious, sporting king, who, as Prince Albert, Duke of York, played at Wimbledon in 1926, was far-travelled and loved by his people. He stayed at Buckingham Palace through the London Blitz, visited all the theatres of war to boost the morale of the forces and toured the worst-bombed areas of Britain while they still burned to comfort the bereaved and homeless. He opened the Festival of Britain in 1951, one of the highlights of the decade. In 1952 his death at 56 stunned the nation. The Coronation of his daughter, Princess Elizabeth, in 1953 was another highlight, and sold another 100,000 television sets. By the end of the decade two-thirds of households had television.

Probably the most characteristic sound in the home in the 1950s was that of light orchestral music, such as the BBC Midland Light Orchestra and, most of all, the Queen's Hall Light Orchestra, which recorded many familiar signature tunes for radio and early television programmes. The decade saw some of the most brilliant exponents of their musical instruments: Winifred Atwell (piano), Earl Bostic (saxophone), Eddie Calvert (trumpet), Les Paul (electric guitar) and Edmundo Ros and his Rumba Band. In popular music in those days you needed a good voice and a good tune to be in the hit parade: the Beverley Sisters, Rosemary Clooney, Perry Como, Bing Crosby, Doris Day, Tab Hunter, Danny Kaye, Frankie Laine, Dean Martin, Vera Lynn, Guy Mitchell, Donald Peers, Jim Reeves, Hank Snow and Tommy Steele spring to mind.

The 1950s launched many famous names and some are still with us – The Archers, David Attenborough, Cliff Richard and Shirley Bassey – while we still celebrate the memory of Tommy Cooper, the Goons, Tony Hancock, Morecambe and Wise, and Elvis Presley.

Only a minority of people had a telephone in the home in 1950. Dad worked for the Post Office Telephones from 1914 to 1949 before he was 'on the phone' himself – and then it was only because there was already a telephone in the house we bought in Wallasey, so we left it there. Our number was Wallasey 655, and the telephone had no dial – we had to lift the receiver and ask the operator for the exchange and number we wanted. People with dials could dial the first three letters of a local exchange name in the days before trunk dialling codes, as there were letters of the alphabet as well as numbers on the dial; the first three letters of each exchange therefore had to be distinctive. In Liverpool city centre, for example, there were Exchange, Maritime and Royal. We still dial ROY (709) for Royal after the area code.

With the shortage of paper lasting long after the war, newspapers, mostly broadsheets, were slim fact-sheets of pithy, objective reports. We did not waste acres of forest on trivial reading matter. Newspapers included the now extinct Daily Dispatch, Daily Graphic/Daily Sketch, Daily Herald and News Chronicle, not forgetting the Children's Newspaper, the Daily Worker and Morning Star. The front pages of The Times and the Liverpool Echo, among others, were still covered with small advertisements in the Victorian tradition.

After the launch of the British aircraft carrier Ark Royal at Birkenhead in 1950 and the Festival of Britain in 1951, there followed a tragic period for news. In December 1951 a column of 24 Royal Marine cadets were killed by a bus in fog in Chatham. In January 1952 we followed the 12-day saga of the sinking American freighter Flying Enterprise under tow to Falmouth, and in the same gale 23 people were killed in an Irish airliner crash in Snowdonia. King George VI died in February, plunging the nation into deep mourning; radio and television closed down except for news bulletins. In August, Lynmouth was destroyed by a torrent of floodwater off Exmoor. In January 1953 the Canadian Pacific liner Empress of Canada was burned out and capsized in Gladstone Dock, Liverpool. Over the weekend of 31 January/1 February 128 people were drowned when the British Railways Stranraer-Larne ferry Princess

Victoria sank in a storm, and the same northerly gale combined with a high spring tide to flood 1,000 miles of the East Coast and 24,000 homes from Grimsby to Deal, and to topple Margate harbour lighthouse into the sea. The flooding drowned 307 people, 2,400 cattle, 520 pigs, more than 12,000 sheep and many more poultry. The Coronation of Princess Elizabeth as Queen in June 1953 lifted the morale of the nation again.

The pictorial general-interest magazines *Everybody's*, *Illustrated* and *Picture Post* disappeared as television took over our homes, and a browse through any old issues of these and of the *Radio Times* gives an insight into life of the period.

The *Eagle* was the flagship new publication that was symbolic of the decade. It was founded and edited by a Southport vicar in 1950 as a part-evangelical, part-educational boys' comic or magazine to counter the violent comics coming out of America. It was produced by Hulton Press and a team of top-link artists, who gave us many well-known fiction characters, notably Dan Dare the space pilot, Captain Pugwash the amiable pirate, and Harris Tweed the eccentric detective. The futuristic designs of Dan Dare's creator, Frank Hampson, seemed to influence the style of utensils, furniture and many other things in that period, while new motor cars of the 1950s – what we call 'classic cars' today – aped the flashy American automobile designs.

Humour of the period, on the other hand, was inclined to quaintness, as were Captain Pugwash and Harris Tweed. Quaintness was the keynote of cartoons and illustrations by Emett, Hoffnung, Jeg, Searle, Sprod, Thelwell and Trog. My favourites were Emett of *Punch* and Trog (Wally Fawkes), creator of Rufus & Flook in the *Daily Mail*. I was brought up on a diet of Rupert, Emett and Trog annuals in the late 1940s and early '50s. Rowland Emett specialised in Edwardiana, gentility, narrow-gauge railways and whimsical machines in his *Punch* cartoons. His drawings were so popular that they were used in Post Office publicity and on stamps, and he translated his drawings into construction of his fantastic inventions in his own forge. He built a quaint railway and a flying machine for the 1951 Festival of Britain gardens in Battersea Park, and continued to build a succession of inventions for exhibitions, culminating in the flying automobile 'Chitty Chitty Bang Bang' in the film of that name in 1967. I have sometimes referred in my text to things being 'Emetty' because they looked quaint, rickety or spindly. Any reader of that era will know what I mean.

Quaintness was also the style of humour in the films of the period, such as those by Walt Disney and Jacques Tati, and the Ealing comedies such as *Passport To Pimlico* (1949), *Whisky Galore* (1949), *The Lavender Hill Mob* (1951), *The Titfield Thunderbolt* (1952) and *The Maggie* (1954). With comedies like this and thrillers like *The Third Man* (1949), *The Blue Lamp*, *King Solomon's Mines* and *Pool Of London* (1950) the British film industry was at its zenith in this period. Professional film-makers recorded the Merseyside scene as the setting for *Waterfront* (1950), *The Magnet* (1950) and *These Dangerous Years* (1957), but there were no Merseyside accents among the actors. Although *Waterfront* was set in the 1930s depression, the locations had not altered. *The Galloping Major* and *The Clouded Yellow* (1951) both ended on Merseyside. *British Movietone News* and *Pathé News* brought us the animated news pictures of the time before television.

I am a product of the late 1940s and early 1950s. I feel like a fish out of water living in the 21st century, not because I am not adaptable – I just don't like it. If I could wake up one morning and look at the calendar and find I was back in 1949 or 1950, I would be a happy man. I would catch the next train to Woodside to find what I would regard as paradise regained. I invite you to come with me, and the pictures in this book show us what we would see.

First impressions last, so the question of approach is paramount in our introduction to new places, which is why I am taking you there by train from Paddington. I have approached Merseyside by sea and from all other points of the compass by road and rail, yet the approach by the Great Western main line to Birkenhead sustains mounting interest and a sense of drama throughout with a sensational finale. The route from Euston is less interesting until we span the Runcorn Gap and descend the Wagnerian cuttings and tunnel to Lime Street on the brink of St George's Plateau, but we can still do that today. The best approach to Liverpool was by ferry from Seacombe, at an oblique angle past the liners at the landing stage, and the best approach to Wallasey was by ferry to New Brighton. The Paddington-Woodside route and Woodside station closed in 1967, so you can no longer buy a return to Woodside. Let me take you along that route to reveal the magic land that lay at the end of the line. To adapt a phrase by singer Gerry Marsden in his 1964 film *Ferry Cross The Mersey*, 'this was the land I loved'. To those who miss it and to those who missed it, this book is dedicated.

WALLASEY was the last steam ferry on the Mersey. She outlasted later steamers of both the Birkenhead and Wallasey fleets built up to seven years after her, and soldiered on as the last steamer in service for 17 months after the *Claughton* on the Woodside run, retiring in May 1963 at the age of 36. She left the Mersey the following February under tow to a breaker's yard at Ghent.

With two years still to run, *Wallasey* is pictured here in 1961 dressed overall to mark the centenary of Wallasey Ferries as a municipal undertaking. She is ploughing her broad wake across the river from Seacombe with the silhouette of New Brighton Tower Building and pier on the horizon astern. Viewed from the promenade deck of a Birkenhead diesel ferry, she is arriving at Liverpool with the Canadian Pacific liner and turbine steamer *Empress of Britain* in the background, having berthed at Prince's Landing Stage that day. The *Empress* (640 feet, 25,585 gross tons) was built on the Tyne in 1956-57, and plied the Liverpool-Greenock-Quebec-Montreal service during the St Lawrence season, and winter cruises from Liverpool and New York. She was sold to the Shaw, Savill & Albion Line in 1970 and scrapped in 1975. Behind the line of tugs at the stage stand the three chimneys of Clarence Dock Power Station.

BIRKENHEAD

Gathering momentum in a volley of steam explosions, the train boomed forth from the smoking, echoing barrels of Paddington's four-arch train shed. In six hours' time it would descend into Woodside station on the Mersey bank at Birkenhead. The smaller but equally grand terminus by the 700-year-old ferry passage across the big river to Liverpool was the northern outpost of the legendary Great Western Railway.

The elegant iron and glass citadel of the old broad-gauge empire was the main departure point from the capital for Birkenhead. There were six down trains and five up trains a day in 1950, but six trains each way for most of the decade, all of 10 to 14 coaches, most of them with restaurant cars or buffet cars; the restaurant car service to Birkenhead ended in 1956. Although the GWR shared Woodside station with the LMS, Euston offered only through carriages once a day each way, hooking off and on the Holyhead train at Chester; otherwise you changed at Crewe or went on to Liverpool.

You could, of course, go by road, but the Crosville express coach service from London took 10 hours and if you missed the 9am departure from Victoria, the next one was at 10.30pm, and that took 9 hours. In an England still innocent of motorways, the coach went by High Wycombe, Oxford, Stratford, Birmingham and Newport (Shropshire) to Birkenhead before diving through the Mersey Tunnel to Liverpool. The Birmingham stop was Erdington tram terminus on the northern outskirts of the city, and you completed your journey to Birmingham by tramcar (until the trams finished in 1953). Few people had motor cars and most of those were middle-aged or wealthy people. In the post-war shortages there was a waiting list to buy a car, and petrol was rationed till 1950. Railway travel in those days was something to be enjoyed rather than endured; it was an essential part of a holiday. So most people went by train, and if you were going to Birkenhead that meant the Great Western.

The railways were nationalised in 1948 and the Paddington-Birkenhead route became part of the Western Region of British Railways, but stations, staff, rolling stock and working practices were unchanged and the Western was particularly traditional. Handsome, Brunswick-green GWR engines, trimmed with brass and copper, with their original brass number-plates, still headed trains of BR 'plum and custard' coaches. The manager at Paddington in the 1950s was a homespun Swindon man who liked to drive the engine to work, and the Great Western was still essentially the Great Western throughout that decade. People still spoke of the Great Western and the LMS, and Grandpa Greenwood from Leicester still referred to the Midland, Great Central and Great Northern of the era before 1923.

God's Wonderful Railway came to Merseyside by the Great Way Round (as the GWR was variously nicknamed), dipping into Wales on the way. It was a much more interesting, scenic route than the LMS route from Euston, and fast trains served 14 towns and villages on the way, although the word 'fast' was qualified by the number of stops, and the journey to Birkenhead took the best part of 6 hours. Birkenhead Woodside was 210¼ miles from London by Great Western; the rival LMS route to Liverpool Lime Street was only 193½ miles. (Railway timetables in those days gave the distances to all stations and halts to the nearest quarter of a mile.) The original Birkenhead route from Paddington, up the Thames valley, from 1854 to 1910, was 229 miles.

Fast through trains ran between Paddington and Birkenhead from 1861 to 1967, reflecting the era of Birkenhead's industrial and commercial importance and business at the docks. The first, on 1 October 1861, was the first standard-gauge train to leave Paddington, stronghold of the broad gauge. It ran on mixed-gauge track from Paddington to Wolverhampton, where, from 1854, passengers had changed trains at the break of gauge. On 7 March 1892 Britain's first corridor train entered service between Paddington and Birkenhead. For the first time 1st, 2nd and 3rd Class passengers could walk to the lavatory and call the guard by electric bell. In 1910 the cut-off route through the Chiltern Hills took 18¾ miles off the journey to Birkenhead. Being on the Great Western also gave Birkenhead through trains from Woodside to Pwllheli and through carriages to Cardiff and Plymouth, and in the summer season through trains ran daily over Southern metals to Margate (till 1959) and Bournemouth (till 1961), a joint operation that brought Southern green coaches to Woodside. These trains followed the old Birkenhead route through the Thames valley.

A journey along the Great Western road to Birkenhead gave us a perspective of Merseyside relative to England and Wales, London and the second city. It was the most dramatic approach to Merseyside by land or sea. The journey was worth making for its own sake, and any Merseyside resident or visitor who never had that experience missed a treat. As we sank into our well-cushioned, soporific seats in our cosy, wood-lined compartment, we eyed the flattened, elongated map of the Great Western Railway centrally placed between the sepia landscapes and seascapes under the rope-net luggage rack. The system radiated west from London with a ramification of branch lines from three trunk routes terminating at three west coast railheads: Penzance, Fishguard and Birkenhead. The line to Birkenhead ran north-west across the Midlands; it was the northern frontier of the system. It looked straight enough on the map, but that was artistic licence; actually it was quite sinuous. Birkenhead was at the top of the map; it was as far as you could go. The Great Western's 95-page guide book to the Paddington-Birkenhead route, published in 1925 as Number Two in the series 'Through the Window', indicates that this line was regarded as second only in importance and scenic interest after the Number One route from Paddington to Penzance.

MERSEY-BOUND

After mixing with the great and the good titled trains to and from the West Country at Paddington and its western approaches, our train, sporting its own route boards above or below the eaves of the carriage roofs, diverged away to the north-west. With a handsome, taper-boilered 'King' or 'Castle' Class pedigree racehorse of the

iron road at the head, we galloped through the rolling Chiltern Hills with their hanging beechwoods. Across the Midland Plateau the irregular patchwork of small, tree-bound fields was seen through the dancing telegraph wires slung from pole to pole along the railway bank and the clouds of steam drifting across the countryside, accompanied by the rhythm of the bogie wheels on the 60-foot lengths of track.

Stations came thick and fast as we echoed through Birmingham and the Black Country, with railway yards, gas-holders, smoke-stacks, church steeples and rooftops as far as the eye could see. The Black Country was truly black – soot-black all over – and its people were all white. I was fascinated by the fantastically weathered slag heaps at the coal mines and a steaming red canal alongside a steelworks. There were stations and halts every 2 miles on average along the main line from Paddington to Woodside. Stations on the Great Western were spacious with wide platforms, wide canopies and ample architectural buildings in local stone, brick or wood, with gas lamps, rock gardens and large, legible station nameboards with white cast-iron capital letters on black boards in white frames. Snow Hill station, Birmingham, had no rock gardens, but it was particularly light and spacious in the Victorian idiom and a hive of steam activity, a fitting halfway stage between Paddington and Woodside. Shrewsbury station was like an Oxford college in Tudor brick and stonework under an overall roof on a viaduct spanning the River Severn and the road north. Gobowen was (and still is) stuccoed Italianate with an arched canopy over the down and bay platforms. The country halts, on the other hand, were short, narrow, wooden platforms with leaning nameboards, Spartan little huts and a few oil lamps.

The old break of gauge at Wolverhampton Low Level was still reflected in a change of engines, as it was the main loco shed and relay point on the route, and a big 'King' had to hand over to a 'Castle' or 'Hall' because of the limited axle-load on bridges. Then we headed west across Shropshire, and the Welsh hills closed in beyond Shrewsbury. This was a scenic diversion as we wound among the Welsh hills and mining villages, spanned the valleys of the River Ceiriog and River

Dee on high viaducts and sojourned at Ruabon and Wrexham, where the symphony of steam railway sounds was punctuated by those musical Welsh voices. .

The drama of the approach to Merseyside began as we rushed downhill to Chester on the Cheshire Plain. The LMS main line from Holyhead swung in from the left and on the four tracks we bridged the Dee again, gaining a better-than-grandstand view of the racecourse from the viaduct with the walled city as a backdrop. In quick succession we passed through the city wall – twice – at the north-west corner, bridged the canal at the foot of the three-lock staircase and were engorged in sheer red-sandstone cuttings and two tunnels, emerging in the great triangle of tracks at the junction with the Birkenhead line and Chester General station. We changed engines again in the shadow of the overall roof of Chester's rambling, arcaded, Italianate station because here the train divided and reversed. The Great Western engine and the leading coaches were uncoupled and usually an LMS engine hooked on to the last eight coaches for the run along the LMS & GW Joint line to Birkenhead, then controlled by both the Midland and Western Regions. From 1951 the Great Western north of Chester was entirely in the Midland Region.

THE APPROACH

Chester was the gateway to the Wirral peninsula, that square-headed promontory of Cheshire jutting west-north-west between the estuaries of the Dee and Mersey. We sprinted along the arrow-straight and level main line from Chester to Birkenhead, drawing nearer to the Mersey bank on our right-hand side. The double track north of Chester spread to four tracks from Ledsham to Birkenhead to cope with the extra traffic on the lines that came in right and left at Hooton from Helsby and West Kirby. The Helsby line served the industries at Ellesmere Port and carried heavy goods traffic between Birkenhead docks and south Lancashire. The four tracks were allocated to fast and slow passenger and goods trains, and four-platform stations flashed past as we bore down the climactic approach to Merseyside.

As housing and industry gathered around us, the jungle of storage tanks and pipes of the Sunlight Soap Works on our right drew aside to reveal an incongruous, unworldly scene. From the railway embankment – kept shorn of bosky growth against fires from sparks – we were treated to a moving panorama of tree-lined avenues of deep-pitched roofs and tall chimneys of picturesque, half-timbered houses and ornate, red-brick cottages in late-Victorian and Edwardian revival styles from Tudor to Art Nouveau, like a town in a fairy tale. This was Port Sunlight, the garden suburb created by William Lever, the first Lord Leverhulme, for his soap factory workers and pensioners between 1888 and 1938. A soap town had to be a clean place for healthy living, and Port Sunlight was, and still is, a showpiece industrial housing estate like Saltaire or Bournville, but not uniform and more rusticated. It stretches for three-quarters of a mile alongside the railway in a quarter-mile-wide belt between the railway and New Chester Road. Port Sunlight was just part of Lever's amazing Sunlight soap empire. The soap works and its allied margarine works on the Mersey bank at Bromborough had their own railway system, dock, fleet of ships and overseas plantations, seed mills, oil depots, railways and river steamers employing a total of 70,000 workers worldwide.

The image of Arcadia passed as abruptly as it had appeared, superseded by the ordinary suburban houses of New Ferry. We entered the County Borough of Birkenhead as we descended a black brick-walled cutting and the brakes went on for the stop at Rock Ferry. Behind the coal sidings on the right just before the station was a yard that always had a few familiar, pre-war Birkenhead blue buses standing together. This was the scrapyard of W. O. Jones in Railway Road, the knacker's yard of many old Birkenhead buses over the years. Surplus steam from the safety valves mushroomed under Bedford Road bridge and we were in Rock Ferry station.

Against the sound of hissing steam, doors slammed and passengers whistled as they alighted from the train and crossed the platform to the vintage wooden electric train waiting in the bay. Rock Ferry station had six platforms and seven tracks spanned by a covered wooden footbridge with four wooden lift towers to all platforms. The three-track bay on the left-hand side was the southern terminus of the Mersey Railway, which burrowed under Birkenhead and the Mersey to Liverpool in a dank, brick-lined tunnel with dimly lit stations. GWR maps showed the main line turning right at Birkenhead and going on to Liverpool, but it never did. The map represented the company's aspiration and pretension, a parcel van and freight barge connection between Birkenhead and Liverpool and the facility for passengers to change at Rock Ferry for the Mersey Railway to Liverpool. Incredibly, in the 1890s the Great Western experimented with running daily return services through the Mersey Railway tunnel from Liverpool Central Low Level to Corwen, to Paddington and to Folkestone Harbour. The Folkestone train, with scheduled connections, was advertised as the Paris train from Liverpool Central! That was in the days of steam on the Mersey Railway and it was done with two or three through GW coaches hauled by the underground railway's own condensing engines, shunting at Rock Ferry for Paddington and again at Reading for Folkestone.

The Mersey Railway was a pioneer of electrification in 1903 and the carriages we saw across the platform at Rock Ferry, which dated from then, looked as if they had been bought second-hand from the old Santa Fe Railway or the New York Elevated, with their rectangular shapes, clerestory roofs and matchboard panels. The pneumatic doors of the electric train slid shut, our guard whistled for the last time, the steam engine whistle responded and the two trains usually left Rock Ferry northbound side by side; nearly every time I travelled this route the steam and electric trains raced north from Rock Ferry. The electrics ran at 10-minute intervals, and the steam train was usually late by the time it got to Rock Ferry; if the driver was a sportsman he would adjust his departure time to race the electric train for the first half-mile till it dived underground at Tranmere. The electric train usually won. But not always.

Streets of terraced houses abutted on to the railway in a succession of gable walls on the right-hand side as we left Rock Ferry. For at least seven years after the war the words 'Welcome home Ted and Les' were painted in large, neat capitals on one gable wall for two Rock Ferry heroes returning from the front. Who were Ted and Les, I wonder; were they the two soldiers we see in battledress in my photograph on Rock Ferry station bridge? Gable ends of terraced houses abutting on to roads and railways were popular sites for advertisements, either painted on the brickwork or printed on poster boards, such as the succession of painted advertisements for Beecham's Pills we had seen on the southern approach to Wrexham.

The last half mile of the journey to Birkenhead was a fitting finale with a sense of drama. From the viaduct over South Tranmere and Lower Tranmere we had a panoramic view of the Mersey and Liverpool. We could see Rock Ferry Pier wading out into the river on our right and, a mile across the water, south Liverpool waterfront from Dingle oil storage tanks along the line of docks to the Pier Head shipping offices with the gigantic red-stone Cathedral crowning the rooftoops of the dense urban ridge rising from the river. By the time we arrived at Birkenhead it was usually afternoon or after dark. By night this scene was lit by a myriad glittering lights, reflected in the river: the lights of the city and of ships riding at anchor in The Sloyne, awaiting high water to enter Birkenhead docks.

The view was eclipsed by the serrated range of high, black sheds and the forest of cranes of Cammell, Laird's shipyard at Lower Tranmere. The train clattered and echoed through the

junctions with lines fanning out on both sides. To the right were the carriage sidings and lines leading to the shipyards and, through a tunnel, to Monks Ferry coaling station for tugs and coasters. To the left were the engine sheds and lines to the gasworks and 'The Sough' (pronounced 'suff'), the four-track goods branch that cut across Birkenhead to the docks in a brick-walled trench below street level. Thus the four-track main line was reduced to two tracks for the last reach to Woodside.

ARRIVAL

We slid through the disused Birkenhead Town station, closed since 1945, on a curve at the mouth of the tunnel under the headland on which Birkenhead stands. With brakes on, the train descended the 1 in 95 gradient of the curving tunnel with hollow tread through 565 yards of Stygian gloom. An electric gong passed the window and flanges squealed as we emerged into daylight – or night gaslight – into the grand, cavernous terminus. Black, rock-faced retaining walls flanked the throat tracks between the tunnel mouth and the twin-arch train shed and the superstructure of a ship (lit up at night) in dry dock peered over the wall at the outer end of the platform on our right. When a ship was floated into or out of the dock, the bows towered high above the station wall and one half expected to hear the station announcer intone, 'The ship standing at platform five is the 11.15 to Rangoon.'

For most of the time I knew it (before British Railways made its modern imprint), Birkenhead Woodside had no station nameboard nor anything to show you had arrived at Birkenhead, except the few station seats with the name BIRKENHEAD WOODSIDE in cast-iron letters screwed on the backrests. Gas lamps hanging from the high roof dangled bits of tin with the name WOODSIDE in white letters on grey. It was rather modest and Emetty. That great, twin-arch roof spanned seven tracks, five wide platforms and a motor road for taxicabs and railway vans between platforms 1 and 2. The platforms could accommodate only eight carriages because space was short between the tunnel mouth and the ferry buildings on the river wall, which was why the train divided at Chester.

Woodside station, by Robert Johnston, was the

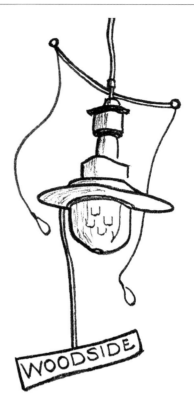

only station on Merseyside to be listed for its architectural interest in the early 1950s, when Victorian railway and industrial buildings were not in vogue. High walls of blind arcading in variegated brickwork with rose windows in the arches surrounded the station on three sides, with a large station clock dial in the wall above the concourse. The Dickensian station offices behind Gothic windows fronted a back service road beside the dry dock with a Gothic-arched iron portico over the loading bay for parcels vans behind the station. The parcels office (designed but not used as the booking hall) was a two-storey chamber with massive timber vaulting springing from ornate stone imposts, and would have done credit as a medieval lord's hall. Pevsner's *Cheshire* described Woodside station, posthumously, as 'one of the few post-1847 buildings of any note in the town centre and one of the few really good main-line termini outside London'.

The station was on a curve and the high side walls and a centre line of ornate cast-iron columns with lacy spandrels supported the lofty, wrought-iron framework of the glazed, twin-arched roof, which echoed to 90 departures and arrivals a day in the 1950s. I can still hear the echoes of slammed carriage doors and the thump-thud of porters unloading mailbags and parcels beneath that cavernous roof in the gas-lit gloom when I used to arrive on the last train from Paddington at 12.19am.

There is an old saying that it is better to travel hopefully than to arrive, suggesting that anticipation is better than realisation, but Birkenhead and Merseyside were no anti-climax. As you walked out of the carriageway arch of the railway station, the wind off the river hit you in the face and your senses were assailed by the strong, salt-sea tang of the Mersey air and by the sights and sounds of the bustling bus station in the angle of the arcaded train shed wall and the long, low, wooden ferry tollhouse with its dormer clock. Men whistled as they went about their business and somewhere under the colonnade an electric gong rang at frequent intervals, perhaps to summon the bus inspector to the telephone.

This was the focal point of Birkenhead; all roads into town funnelled into here. Chester Street and Hamilton Street disgorged blue Birkenhead town buses and green Crosville country buses – pre-war, war-time and post-war Leylands, Guys, Daimlers and Bristols – that rattled down the slope of the Mersey bank, swept around the horseshoe turn by the ferry tollhouse and laboured back up the slope and away. Half of the buses stopped to drop their passengers at the glazed, iron colonnade of the ferry tollhouse, then took up their stands at shelters alongside the train shed wall or on loading islands facing uphill. The rest set down and picked up passengers at kerbside and island shelters facing the ferry, then leaned over as they accelerated through the turn by the tollhouse and away up the slope. Some older Birkenhead buses grunted up the slope into town with NORTH CIRCLE on their destination blinds; to my boyish, romantic mind this had connotations of the Arctic Circle. Where was the North Circle, I wondered. Beyond the 'ultima Thule' of Birkenhead Woodside anyway – I had visions of the buses returning with icicles. Later I found that the North Circle bus route embraced the two contrasting sides of Birkenhead: the slums and industry of dockland and the villadom west and south of the park.

All this animation and activity at Woodside, combined with the view from up the slope or down on the river wall beside the tollhouse across the Mersey shipping lanes to Liverpool's noble waterfront – one of the most stirring sights in Britain – gave one the feeling of having arrived, and that this was the place to be. The ferry, bus and railway terminus at Woodside was, however, a place where everyone was passing through to somewhere else, so we moved on. While others filed past into the echoing railway station, we went by ferry to Liverpool and perhaps on to New Brighton, or we took a bus to the outer reaches of Birkenhead or across the docks to Wallasey.

THE TOWNSCAPE

Seen from the top deck of a ferry steamer off Woodside landing stage, Birkenhead rose in cliffs of late-Georgian and post-Georgian buildings in stucco and blackened stone on the crest of the slope above the ferry landing place and beside the twin-arch train shed. The skyline was dominated by the green-cupola'd, black, classical clock tower of the Town Hall, the Italianate hydraulic tower to work the lifts at Hamilton Square underground station on the Mersey Railway, and the 270-foot smoke-stack of the Mersey Railway power station on the corner of Hamilton Street and Canning Street. The only skyscrapers were the three 1930s Art Deco brick ventilation towers of the Mersey road tunnel, notably the 210-foot tower on the river bank by the ferry landing stage. To the left of the tower stretched the flat no-man's-land of the docks, a mile across at the river wall and reaching 2 miles inland, dividing Wallasey from Birkenhead. Halfway across the docks rose the tall, slender, Italianate hydraulic tower that powered the dock gates, swing-bridges, hoists and capstans.

Giant brick granaries and mills bordered the Wallasey side of the East Float and the Birkenhead side of the West Float.

The redeeming feature of this industrial townscape was the backdrop. The birch woods that once covered Birkenhead and Woodside still clothe the continuous line of Bidston Hill (238 feet), Oxton Ridge (230 feet) and Prenton Ridge (259 feet). This wooded ridge runs north to south right across the back of the town. Until the mid-20th century it formed a watershed between town and country, with the sylvan villa suburbs of Claughton, Oxton and Prenton nestling on its slopes. A spur of this ridge runs nearer the river culminating in Tranmere Hill (180 feet), which projects right into the town. Church Road, Higher Tranmere, runs along the spine of this ridge, its narrow, winding course and small shops retaining something of the character of the old Tranmere village street. Side streets dropping away gave glimpses of high views over the gulf of the Mersey, with Lower Tranmere shipyard cranes on the near side and Liverpool's southern docks on the far side.

As the road dived off the north end of the ridge, an amazing bird's eye panorama of Birkenhead opened up before us. As we swung down through the reverse curves of Pearson Road we saw first the shipyards on our right, then the railway yards, engine sheds, two giant gas-holders and the rooftops, towers and smoke-stacks of the whole of central Birkenhead hove into view. They all came up to meet us as we swooped down the steep, straight pitch of Argyle Street South like an aircraft landing in the middle of town, with Argyle Street stretching ahead in a straight line like a runway across the central business district. I envied the Edwardians the thrill of riding open-top tramcars down that gradient, which was considered too steep for motorbuses to climb (they attained Higher Tranmere via Borough Road and Whetstone Lane). Pearson Road was built for the Tranmere trams in 1901 and named after the Chairman of the Corporation Tramways Committee, H. Laird Pearson. It was cut out of the rocky hillside on a gradient of 1 in 13½, with two double-bends, retaining walls and embankments, to by-pass the 1 in 7 gradient at the top of Argyle Street South.

THE TOWN CENTRE

At the foot of the hill, less than 100 yards past the Tranmere/Birkenhead marker signs, we were alongside Birkenhead Central station on the Mersey Railway in the central business district of Birkenhead, which was set around five squares. Central station faced a triangular open space at the crossing of Argyle Street and Borough Road with a noble clock tower in Portland stone in gardens in the angle of Clifton Crescent and off-duty Corporation buses standing casually around an asphalt plain in the angle of Wilbraham Street. A long cast-iron and glass colonnade around the full length of the station frontage doubled as a shelter for bus stops right around the bend from Borough Road into Argyle Street South.

A short length of Borough Road led us into a chain of three irregularly shaped wide open spaces. Haymarket and Market Place South were surrounded by a medley of Italianate, Victorian Gothic and Edwardian buildings. King's Square, named after King George V, who opened the Mersey road tunnel in 1934, was formally laid out as the monumental main tunnel entrance: a splash of white Portland stone and flower gardens in the smoke-blackened heart of old Birkenhead.

As we filed through Argyle Street from Central station or along Hamilton Street from Haymarket through the central business district towards Woodside, we became aware of late-Georgian and matching post-Georgian stone buildings, some with rounded or canted corners, and similar classical terraces in the cross streets, like the buildings we had seen at the top of the slope above the ferry, then suddenly we found ourselves passing along one side of a spacious, dignified Georgian square. It was so incongruous in the general context of Birkenhead that it was like a vision, but it explained all the fragments of Georgian townscape we had seen so far. Here on the brink of the slope down to the ferry and the docks was Hamilton Square: 6 acres of public gardens surrounded by wide carriageways and a quadrangle of trim, uniform terraces of four-storey houses, now offices, with finely dressed (ashlar) stone facades, dominated by the Town Hall with its tall clock tower and Corinthian portico, centrally placed between terraces on one side of the square. All the buildings were black with soot, some of the houses were veiled in ivy, and the white cenotaph in front of the Town Hall was a nice foil against the black. The late-Georgian domestic architecture is a dour north-British style reminiscent of the Georgian sector of Edinburgh and other Scottish burghs, but the open aspect of the gardens, with few trees to mask the panorama of the terraces combined with the presence of the Town Hall, is a masterpiece of townscaping, and humble Birkenhead has what is rated as one of the finest squares in Europe.

In the mid-20th century British double-deck buses and trams, with their local identities in body styles, liveries and legends, were an important element of the townscape. Birkenhead's post-war Massey-bodied, Gardner-engined buses, with their smooth, curved outlines in mid-blue and cream and their deep rumble and gear whine, plying along three sides of Hamilton Square in the 1950s, befitted the dignity of the square in a way that no other buses have done before or since.

Hamilton Square is an oasis of old Birkenhead – a genteel Birkenhead of its pre-industrial past, a nascent Birkenhead dating from the 1820s, when the first steam ferries brought Liverpool's wealthier ship-owners and merchants across the river to retreat to this undeveloped, rural headland and built villas and a hotel with gardens sloping down to the river. The square, the town plan and the town's chief industry – shipbuilding – had a dual Scottish authorship. William Laird (1780-1841), from Greenock, was a Liverpool ship-owner who in 1824 set up the Birkenhead Iron Works, a boiler factory, on the shore of the tidal creek Wallasey Pool at what is now the end of Livingstone Street, and in 1828 he began building ships at what is now Gill Brook Basin.

THE GRID

Laird bought a large area of farmland and engaged one of Edinburgh New Town's surveyors and architects, James Gillespie Graham, to plan a new town and design Hamilton Square, which is why the rectangular street plan, known as 'the grid', and the houses in the square are similar to Georgian Edinburgh. Hamilton Square, named after one of the chief architects of Edinburgh New Town, was begun in 1826 and completed in the 1840s in a

uniform late-Georgian or Regency style, which continued long after the death of King George IV in 1830, through the reign of William IV and well into the early Victorian era. I call it post-Georgian as it was still Georgian in concept, style and proportions, but it merged into the Italianate. The Scottish authorship of the original plan bequeathed us the names Hamilton Street, Argyle Street, Douglas Street, Duncan Street and Camperdown Street, and in this area we find isolated buildings and terraces of similar style, built mainly in the 1840s.

Hamilton Square was the cornerstone of the grid street layout, the starting point for all the parallel and rectangular lines of streets, which extended for a mile from Chester Street to Duke Street in a quarter-mile-wide strip between the shafts of Conway Street and Cleveland Street. Birkenhead Improvement Commissioners, forerunners of the Borough Council, were elected in 1833 and extended Laird's grid plan north-east along the dockside and north-west for a further three-quarters of a mile in an area tapering from Duke Street to St James's Church. It was intended to build the whole of this area in the same style and elegance as the terraces of Hamilton Square. The main streets of the grid were laid out 50 and 60 feet wide between the building lines, as we see in the pictures of Cleveland Street and Cathcart Street; a crescent with gardens was laid out off Camden Street and some of the rectangular plots would have become more squares with gardens. It would have been one of Britain's classical towns. A few more isolated stone terraces were built in the streets around Hamilton Square in the 1830s and '40s, but not to the same standard as Graham's prototype.

Alas for 'the best laid plans of mice and men', the developers ran out of money and the marked layout of streets lay undeveloped and overgrown for many years. Laird's ironworks and shipyard and his plan for docks was not compatible with a town for gentry, and the grid layout of streets was eventually built up, from 1847, with mean terraced houses for the thousands of workers engaged in building the new town, developing and manning the shipyards and docks, and working in the many ancillary factories and service industries interspersed among the houses in these streets.

The spaces left between the main streets for large private gardens were filled in with back streets and alleyways.

Whichever way you went from Hamilton Square, the image faded, especially if you headed north-west into the grid along Price Street or Cleveland Street, stretching straight, wide and level to the horizon through this drab urban desert of two- and three-storey terraced houses fronting straight on to the streets, punctuated by public houses, factories and storage yards. The docks lay down a slope on the right-hand flank but only a quarter of a mile from the docks across this grid, at the outer end of Conway Street, Birkenhead springs another of its surprises.

A large Ionic triumphal arch in red sandstone stands at the corner of Birkenhead Park, 226 acres of landscape gardening, which, since its opening in 1847, has mellowed and now looks quite natural with its great trees, hillocks and irregularly shaped pools and islets. A winding carriage drive around the park is dotted with Victorian villas in Gothic, Jacobean and Italianate architecture in brick and stone. This setting, with its many sporting facilities, is also the battleground of Birkenhead Park RUFC with its stadium on Park Road North, where the grim grid is fronted by more respectable terraced houses in Ruabon pressed brick with bay windows, small front gardens and pleasant views across the park.

CLAUGHTON TO BEBINGTON

Nowhere could the contrast in the urban environment 'on the other side of the park' have been more marked than in Birkenhead. To the north of the park lay the barracks of dockland. To the south and west the land sloped up towards the wooded ridge and we were in suburban Claughton with quiet, wide streets between grey, stone walls in tunnels of trees that masked more large Victorian villas, mainly Italianate, in brick, stucco and stone, some of which had been converted to private schools and colleges. The Victorianised old centre of Oxton, if you could find it, off the beaten track, retained something of its village character and, in the leafy outer edges of Claughton, Oxton, Prenton and Higher Bebington, ranged below the top of the ridge, the much-maligned Birkenhead

has some of the most beautiful residential suburbs anywhere in Britain.

A characteristic feature of the Birkenhead townscape and suburbs were the cast-iron colonnades with glazed roofs and fascias that spanned the full width of the footpaths at bus stops (such as we see in Cleveland Street from Hamilton Square), usually with wooden park bench seats, affording ample shelter from the rain not only for waiting passengers but also for passers-by. Their fascias carried the words 'Birkenhead Corporation Motors' in white glass on the plain glass panels, and the ironwork was painted blue like the buses.

The most secluded residential area of Birkenhead was Rock Park, with its toll lodges. Ashlar classical villas and stuccoed Italianate villas stood in large grounds and undulating woodland shelving to a private Esplanade with a red sandstone retaining wall lapped by the river south of Rock Ferry Pier. The estate was built by the Royal Rock Ferry Company between 1836 and 1850. Rock Park and its Esplanade stretched for half a mile along the Mersey bank from Rock Ferry Pier to the abutment in the river wall from which New Ferry Pier once strode into the river. New Ferry had closed when the pier was rammed by a coaster in fog in 1922 and dismantled, but the small, sturdy, brick tollhouse was still there on the abutment and made somebody a nice little bungalow. This was the southernmost building in the County Borough of Birkenhead. Beyond it New Ferry Road curved up into the nondescript town of New Ferry in the municipal Borough of Bebington to the town centre at the Toll Bar on New Chester Road. Over the Toll Bar the road continued past Port Sunlight to semi-detached Bebington, where the Birkenhead suburbs ended in undulating, wooded country.

ROCK FERRY

Rock Ferry Pier and waterfront was one of my favourite haunts on Merseyside. Here was the ghost of a quaint little riverside resort with its hotel, pier, bath-house, esplanade and a small patch of sandy beach – although half the pier deck was in ruins, the bath-house had been converted to cottages, the esplanade was a rough track and nobody would want to swim from the beach

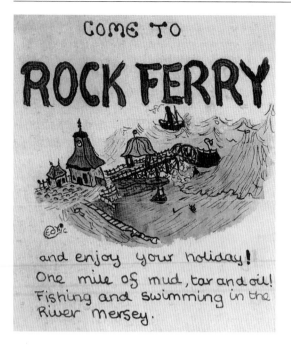

COME TO

ROCK FERRY

and enjoy your holiday!
One mile of mud, tar and oil!
Fishing and swimming in the
River Mersey.

because of the murky, oily water and the muddy foreshore. I was interested to find in my 1904 Bartholomew's *Gazetteer Of The British Isles* that Rock Ferry was a 'favourite summer resort' in Edwardian times. Later I read that the Royal Rock Hotel, the cornerstone and social centre of Rock Park by the pier entrance, had 'pleasure gardens' and tea gardens and provided entertainment in a marquee in the early 20th century.

The old ferry slipway of 1820, built of megalithic blocks of red sandstone, sloped into the river along the south side of the pier, with a paved runway for horse-drawn vehicles using the ferry. It is still used by fishermen and yachtsmen with dinghies to get to their fishing-boats and yachts moored out in the river. The end of the slipway was demolished to make way for the floating landing stage at the end of the pier, built to replace the slipway in 1899.

The ferry had closed in 1939 but the iron pier was still open for tugmen, fishermen, yachtsmen and promenaders. The clock on the tollhouse had stopped, but we still walked under the glazed colonnade into the tollhouse and bought 1d cardboard ferry tickets from a dimly lit booking office. Out along the wooden deck of the pier we viewed with awe the ruined state of the decking along the right-hand side, over the centre railing that once divided the landing passengers from the

embarking passengers. That half of the pier was closed to save maintenance costs and was the location of 'the old pier' in the 1950 film *The Magnet*.

Down on the landing stage was the old ferry navigation light and fog bell tower, and one of the two arched-roof wooden shelters was still there, converted to a store shed. To complete the picture a steam tug was usually tied up at the old ferry berth. On the deck of the landing stage were the dinghies of fishermen and yachtsmen. Both the Royal Mersey Yacht Club (founded in 1844) and the Tranmere Sailing Club were quartered at Rock Ferry and kept their yachts moored in The Sloyne anchorage offshore between New Ferry and Tranmere.

From the relative tranquillity of Rock Ferry Pier head and landing stage we had a front-seat down-river view of the busy Mersey shipping lanes between Tranmere shipyards and Liverpool's waterfront shipping offices. Up-river the Mersey widened out to a breadth of 3 miles between Ellesmere Port and Speke airport, and the great hills of the Delamere Forest at Helsby and Frodsham closed off the view, which looked like a great inland lake in Wales. In those declining years of Rock Ferry this was a peaceful scene on a sunny summer's day. At low tide one could hear the mud popping in the warmth of the sun. Here at Rock Ferry was a living vestige of Birkenhead history in the throes of death.

HISTORY

Birkenhead was entirely a 19th-century creation, while neighbouring Wallasey dated from the 5th century and Liverpool from the 13th century. But Birkenhead has the most interesting history of the three: the survival of its medieval priory and ferry to the present day, the dual Scottish authorship of the new town, its classical, Georgian concept and beginnings, the complete transformation from agriculture to industry within 40 years, the thousand-fold increase in its population between 1801 and 1901 and, within this revolution, Thomas Brassey's Canada Works and the pioneer enterprises that were an important contribution to civilisation.

Until the 19th century Birkenhead was a birch-wooded headland with low red-sandstone cliffs and a rocky shore jutting into the Mersey between two tidal creeks, Tranmere Pool and Wallasey Pool. A 100-foot-long Roman bridge of timber beams on stone piers down to bedrock was unearthed in silt during dock and railway construction in 1850 at Bridge End at the end of Bridge Street, indicating that the Romans had used the ancient trackway leading from the Mersey crossing at Woodside to the High Lake (Hoylake) anchorage at Meols. The bridge crossed the mouth of what was later called Bridge End Brook where it flowed into Wallasey Pool at Bridge End Farm. This also indicates that there might have been a Mersey ferry passage at Woodside in Roman times.

Another trackway led from Woodside to Chester, and in the 12th century a small priory for 16 monks was built on the headland close to the packhorse trail and the river crossing. The Benedictine monks cared for wayfarers and had a work ethic in farming, hospitality, roads, bridges and ferries. They also had a granary in Liverpool, a fishing village, which in the 13th century grew to a small market town with a coastal trade and a castle. The monks of Birkenhead worked a free ferry passage to Liverpool from the shore where the packhorse trails from Chester and Meols met at Woodside. The earliest record of the existence of this monastic ferry is dated 1282, but Liverpool boatmen also improvised ferries for travellers from the other side.

The ferry boat, driven by oar and sail, plied irregularly on this mile-long passage across this wide, swift 'arm of the sea' only when travellers required it and the weather and tide permitted it. In accordance with their order, the monks also provided free hospitality at the priory for travellers waiting for the tide and weather to cross the river. Woodside Ferry and the remains of Birkenhead Priory are still with us today, and the Chapter House (a 12th-century priory chapel with a 14th-century scriptorium above) is the oldest intact building on Merseyside.

King Edward I visited the priory in 1275 and again in 1277, when he held court there for five days on his way to his successful campaign to subdue and annex Wales (1277-83). In 1318 King Edward II authorised the monks to charge for hospitality and build a guest-house for the increasing number of travellers waiting to cross the river. This was endorsed by a charter of King Edward III in 1330, which also gave the monks and their successors legal ferry rights on this passage and allowed them to charge tolls. Woodside Ferry was now part of the King's highway. The priory closed in 1536 and the headland and ferry rights passed to the Crown, then, from 1545, to a succession of land-owners, who rebuilt the monastic guesthouse as Birkenhead Hall next to the priory ruins.

In the Civil War the Cavaliers garrisoned Birkenhead Hall and fired cannon-shot across the river at Liverpool when it was held by the Roundheads. Birkenhead Hall was taken by the Roundheads and razed in 1644, but was rebuilt by the squire after the war.

Stagecoaches came to Birkenhead from 1762. The coach road from Chester came through Lower Bebington and Tranmere via what are now Church Road, Whetstone Lane, Grange Road and Chester Street. In 1790 an embankment was thrown across Tranmere Pool to divert the coach road from Tranmere Hill to what is now Old Chester Road and Green Lane, and in 1833 that route was by-passed by the New Chester Road, built straight from Bromborough to Lower Tranmere. The Woodside Royal Mail Ferry Hotel was the traditional coach terminus at Birkenhead. Coaches also ran to New Ferry, Rock Ferry and Tranmere Ferry, and the Royal Mail contract shifted between Woodside, Tranmere and Rock Ferry, leaving us the names Royal Rock Hotel and Royal Castle Hotel (Tranmere Ferry entrance was a castellated folly). The present Woodside Hotel, built in 1833-34, was the coach terminus until the coming of the Birkenhead Railway in 1840. Coaches ran from Woodside daily to Holywell, Bangor, Welshpool, Holyhead, Shrewsbury, Birmingham and London. Holywell was a round trip in a day, Birmingham took one day and London two.

By the beginning of the 19th century Liverpool had grown to a teeming, industrial slum city with five docks, while on the opposite bank of the river Birkenhead was still a peaceful rural headland between two creeks with five farmsteads, a pattern of fields and woods, the squire's hall, the priory ruins, a ferry slipway, the Chester coach road and

Grange Lane, the track worn by the monks to their grange (a monastic farm and granary) at Claughton. The population of Birkenhead was 110 at the first national census in 1801, when Liverpool's was 77,653. At that time Neston was the largest township in Wirral, with 1,486 people, and Tranmere was the second largest with 353 people. In the 1811 census there were still only 105 people in Birkenhead. It was the advent of steam ferries providing reliable, regular services from Liverpool to Birkenhead from 1820 that was the catalyst for the initial residential development of Birkenhead, and the population grew from 200 in 1821 to 2,569 in 1831.

The nascent town developed around two growth centres by the two ferries that now plied to the headland: the old ferry at Woodside on the corner of Wallasey Pool and the new Birkenhead Ferry, which opened with a steam service in 1820 (two years before Woodside Ferry turned to steam) and landed at the new Birkenhead Hotel by the hall and the priory ruins on the corner of Tranmere Pool. The hotel, which opened in 1819, became a coach terminus and a social centre. It stood on the clifftop overlooking the river with tea gardens, a stone slipway and a small, tidal basin at the south end of Church Street. Villas were built along the south end of Church Street, St Mary's Church was built in Priory Street in 1819-21, and the town centre of Birkenhead grew up around a nest of slum alleys and courtyards at the junction of Chester Street and Grange Lane (later Grange Street).

In this area the Birkenhead Railway terminated at Grange Lane in 1840, the Market Hall opened in 1845 and the post-Georgian shopping centre, Market Cross, opened on the corner of Chester Street and Market Street in 1847. Before the end of the 19th century, however, the shopping district moved from Chester Street up Grange Road (a continuation of Grange Street on the line of the old Grange Lane) and the railway was extended in tunnel under the headland to Woodside Ferry in 1878. The small, classical Grange Lane terminal building survived till 1968.

Writing in his book *The Mersey, Ancient & Modern* in 1878 of his first visit to Merseyside in 1825, Benjamin Blower described Woodside as 'a small village in the district of Birkenhead'. Whitewashed cottages among trees are depicted in a painting of the ferry slipway in 1814. Short terraces of Georgian houses faced in stone, brick or stucco were built in the 1820s and '30s around the north-east corner of Hamilton Square, at the north end of Chester Street and Church Street and on a supplementary grid of streets laid out on the slope between Cleveland Street and Wallasey Pool along the axis of Bridge Street. The isolated terraces that dotted the headland in the 1820s gradually spread until, by the 1850s, the two areas of development joined up and Woodside became a district of the new town of Birkenhead.

THE INDUSTRIAL AGE

The chief factor for the industrial development of Birkenhead was the opening of the docks in 1847 to relieve the overcrowding of Liverpool docks, and this date was a turning point in the development of Birkenhead from Graham's classical design to industrial buildings, cheap mass housing and the prodigious growth of the population from 8,225 in 1841 to 24,285 in 1851 and 42,997 in 1871. The new labour came largely from famine-stricken Ireland. In 1877 Birkenhead became a municipal borough (a second-tier authority under Cheshire County Council), taking in Claughton, Oxton, Tranmere and Rock Ferry. The town became an independent county borough in 1888. By 1901 the population had grown from 110 to 110,915 in 100 years. Birkenhead was a product of the Steam Age.

The profile of the promontory was lost as the docks sealed the mouth of Wallasey Pool from 1844 to 1866 and Tranmere Pool was reclaimed first for the Chester turnpike road in 1790, then for the railway and the gasworks in 1840, and finally for the shipbuilding yards after Tranmere Ferry closed in 1904. Dock construction in Wallasey Pool caused Laird's shipyard to move to the Mersey bank north of Tranmere Pool in 1856. It was still called Birkenhead Iron Works, but in 1903 Laird Brothers amalgamated with Sheffield steel-plate-makers Charles Cammell & Company to form Cammell, Laird & Company, and between 1904 and 1918 the new firm extended south across the mouth of Tranmere Pool to cover 108 acres of reclaimed land with 1,033 yards of riverfront. Now the shoreline of Birkenhead was a straight river wall, broken by slipways, dock gates and landing stages.

Another industrial giant of Birkenhead, besides William Laird and his son John, was the legendary Thomas Brassey (1805-70). This Cheshire farmer's son from Bulkeley became the world's greatest civil engineering contractor, based at Birkenhead, and he lived here in Whetstone Lane for many years when he was not visiting construction sites. He started with a brick and lime works on Wallasey Pool at the end of Cathcart Street in the 1830s. He built New Chester Road in 1833 and progressed to building docks, railways and bridges all over the world, supplying the artisans, labour and hardware shipped out from Birkenhead. Brassey built one-third of all railways in Britain, one-quarter of French railways and, in all, one mile in every 20 of the world's railways in Europe, Asia, Africa, India, Australia and North and South America.

He set up the Canada Works (off what is now Beaufort Road) in 1853 for the construction of the Grand Trunk Railway for 539 miles from Quebec to Toronto, including the 2-mile Victoria Bridge across the St Lawrence River at Montreal. At a time when Britain was the 'workshop of the world', Brassey had to supply the navvies, carpenters, bricklayers, masons and steel erectors, and the Canada Works produced the prefabricated ironwork for bridges, the steam shovels, the railway track, locomotives, carriages and wagons. The works were highly mechanised for their time and their products were made to the highest standards. The Canadian project is remembered in the name of the Grand Trunk Hotel in Old Bidston Road.

After Brassey died, Canada Works became W. A. Stevens's shipbuilding yard and built, among other things, the 600-foot ferry landing stage at Liverpool (George's Stage) of 1874-75, the Wallasey cattle stage on the dock wall between Woodside and Seacombe in 1876, the first Seacombe ferry landing stage in 1879, a Woodside goods ferry (the iron paddle-steamer *Tranmere*) in 1884, a Woodside passenger ferry (the steel twin-screw steamer *Cheshire*) in 1889, and rebuilt New Ferry landing stage in 1889. Canada Works shut down shortly after that and the site was occupied by Vernon's mills and silos, but the name lives on in Canada Creek, a basin on the south side of the West Float. George's Landing Stage survived in use till 1973.

For a town that was a late starter in history, Birkenhead was still a pioneer in some notable spheres. Laird's shipyard was the first to be tooled up for the construction of iron ships, and launched its first iron paddle-steamer in 1833, the first trans-Atlantic screw-steamer in 1838, and the world's first steel ship in 1858. The Birkenhead Improvement Commissioners were enterprising in commissioning Britain's leading landscape gardener, Sir Joseph Paxton, to design Birkenhead Park, and his pupil, Edward Kemp, to supervise the work of what was, when it opened in 1847, the first municipal public park in the world. They also commissioned the American shipping agent, railway promoter and entrepreneur George Train to build the Birkenhead Street Railway, the first tramway in Britain, which opened in 1860 between Birkenhead Park and Woodside Ferry. It took only 14 weeks in gestation, including six weeks for 59 men to lay the 2¼ miles of paved street track; meanwhile the first four ornate horse-cars were prefabricated in America and assembled at Birkenhead.

Another American, George Starbuck, began the first tramcar factory outside America at Vittoria Wharf, Birkenhead, in 1862. His Starbuck Car & Wagon Company in Cleveland Street (1872-86) built horse-trams for Birkenhead and other tramways at home and overseas, and several still survive in museums. The oldest extant tramcars in Britain are all Starbuck horse-cars: an 1871 Ryde Pier tram in Hull Transport Museum, an 1873 Porto tram and an 1874 Sheffield tram in the National Tramway Museum, Crich, and an 1876 Birkenhead tram in Woodside Ferry tollhouse.

Birkenhead also saw trials and demonstrations of self-contained steam tramcars built by Starbuck and by Allan & Dickinson, also of Cleveland Street. The Starbuck company secretary, George Milnes, continued production of tramcar bodies and trucks in Cleveland Street into the pioneer electric traction era, and Milnes cars of the 1890s still work the Manx Electric Railway today. Milnes and Daimler built the pioneer British motor buses in 1902. That year Milnes moved his works to Hadley, Shropshire, and his son continued production of tramcar accessories at the third tramcar works in

Cleveland Street, G. C. Milnes, Voss. This firm also built the body on a pioneer trolleybus, which was tried on Cleveland Street in 1909.

In 1908 the worldwide Boy Scout movement was founded by Sir Robert Baden-Powell, speaking at Birkenhead YMCA in Grange Road, and the 1st and 2nd Birkenhead Scout Troops, formed at that time, were the first scout troops in the world. To mark the 21st anniversary of the movement, the first World Scout Jamboree was held at Birkenhead's Arrowe Park in 1929, attended by 50,000 scouts from 72 countries. The 1st Birkenhead Troop disbanded about 1990; the 2nd Troop – although it suspended activities for the Second World War – is now the oldest scout troop in the world.

Cammell, Laird's shipyard was at its peak from the late 1930s to the late 1950s and employed more than 10,000 men when the stocks were full. To their credit they had a tradition of getting the

contracts to build warships and submarines for the Royal Navy and foreign navies. They launched Britain's first purpose-built aircraft carrier, *Ark Royal*, in 1937, built 106 vessels for the Royal Navy during the Second World War, and the new *Ark Royal* in 1950. The Tranmere yard also launched the largest ships ever built in England in their time: the Cunard White Star liner *Mauretania* in 1938 and the Union Castle liner *Windsor Castle* in 1959, the last liner built in England.

By the mid-20th century, the time of our review, the County Borough of Birkenhead extended over the ridge into the rural hinterland to take in the villages of Bidston, Prenton, Upton, Woodchurch and Thingwall and had a population of 142,392 at the 1951 census.

This was Birkenhead. It was not as romantic, perhaps, as those other Great Western railheads, Fishguard and Penzance, but much more interesting and full of surprises.

THE GREAT WESTERN ROAD TO BIRKENHEAD: A Paddington to Birkenhead train changes engines at Wolverhampton Low Level, the relay point at the old break of gauge. Former Great Western Railway (GWR) locomotive No 4903 *Aston Hall* (right) moves forward to take over from No 6000 *King George V* at the head of the train and take it on to Chester. A Pannier tank reverses under the shadow of

Wednesfield Road bridge and a Wolverhampton Corporation bus, crossing overhead, is seen between the clouds of steam. Although this picture was taken in 1960, 12 years into the British Railways era, all three locomotives were of Great Western pedigree, as were the water column, the semaphore signal and the signal cabin beyond the bridge.

Above These houses in Park Road, **PORT SUNLIGHT**, were built in 1892-95 in one of the vernacular revival styles of the period and exemplify the picturesque beauty of this soap works garden suburb of Birkenhead. The founder, William Lever (1851-1925), a philanthropist with an interest in town planning and architecture, established his Sunlight soap works at the end of the 19th century on 91 acres between Bromborough Pool, a navigable creek of the Mersey, and the railway main line between Bebington and New Ferry. With the great vision of late-Victorian entrepreneurs he transformed a further 130 acres of marsh, scrub and slums into this residential paradise for the workers. Built between 1888 and 1938, the 871 houses are in 68 terraced groups, each of a different design in a variety of vernacular styles on an irregular layout, landscaped by public gardens and trees. The company also provided utilities and public buildings, including a school, a 1,000-seat non-denominational church and one of the finest art galleries in Britain. Lever employed 25 eminent architects and practices, and the first nine houses in this 1939 picture were designed by William Owen of Warrington. The projecting group beyond was by Douglas & Fordham of Chester. Both groups are in the neo-Tudor/Elizabethan half-timbered style favoured on this estate. The opposite side of Park Road lies across the landscaped parkland of The Dell, the valley of a former stream that drained into Bromborough Pool. *Judges' Ltd postcard*

Below The spacious open parkland that offsets the housing in Port Sunlight culminates in a broad swath of gardens in a grand, central avenue leading up to the **LADY LEVER ART GALLERY** at the focal point of the estate. This low, domed, classical building in Portland stone by Segar Owen was built in 1914-22 to house William Lever's own collection of paintings, pottery, furniture and sculpture, and was named in memory of his wife, who died before him. It is one of the finest art collections in Britain. The 364-foot-long building has Ionic porticoes facing north, south, east and west, but this 1950 view shows the main entrance, facing south to the fountain and central gardens. *Valentine's postcard*

Above All Mersey-bound road traffic from London, the Black Country and Wales came this way along **NEW CHESTER ROAD, NEW FERRY**, the A41 trunk road through the town centre on the approach to Birkenhead and the Mersey Tunnel. There was no by-pass, no motorway and no road across Runcorn Gap. There were delays at Widnes Transporter Bridge and the next crossing up-river was at Warrington. Although New Ferry was in the suburban Borough of Bebington, the older, closely knit built-up area of Birkenhead began here. Birkenhead Tramways had a terminus and depot here from 1877 to 1931 and this was the point where Crosville country buses exchanged passengers with Birkenhead Corporation trams and buses until the through-running agreement in 1930.

New Chester Road was built straight and wide from Bromborough to Lower Tranmere in 1833 by the famous Birkenhead civil engineering contractor Thomas Brassey, to by-pass the gradients and bottlenecks of the old Chester road through Lower Bebington and Dacre Hill. The new road was a turnpike with a toll-gate at this crossroads, which is still called New Ferry Toll Bar today, though tolls were lifted in 1883. The toll cottage stood where the Midland Bank stands (left) on the south corner of Bebington Road. The Westminster Bank stands on the north corner of Bebington Road, which leads to Bebington & New Ferry station and Bebington Town Hall. New Ferry Road (right) leads down to the site of the ferry pier.

The canopied shops are those of George Mason, family grocer (left), H. Wolfe & Son, house furnishers, and W. H. Edge & Son, butchers (right). The driveway on this side of the shop led through an arched alley to the butcher's own slaughterhouse at the back.

Cars in this 1954 view are, on the left, a 1949 Morris Minor and a 1935 Hillman Minx in a line of northbound vehicles waved on by a policeman on a pedestrian crossing. A Seddon lorry heads a line of southbound vehicles and two Birkenhead buses can be seen in the background, one of them emerging from New Ferry Depot. As there was nowhere for buses to turn round on the streets of New Ferry, those on route 10 from New Brighton terminated by looping through the depot with the passengers aboard and unloading just inside the south portal.

Below Only 500 yards from the hurly-burly of New Chester Road there was peace on **THE WATERFRONT** at New Ferry. The former ferry buildings still stood on the abutment in the Mersey wall where the pier once strode into the river. The existence of the New Ferry passage to Liverpool was first recorded in 1774, together with a coach connection to Chester. The 850-foot-long pier was built in 1865 by James Brunlees, better known for his piers at Southport and Southend (he was also the engineer for the Mersey Railway tunnel). Birkenhead Corporation took over the ferry, together with Rock Ferry, in 1897, and New Ferry steamers called at Rock Ferry. While the town of New Ferry (including the houses in this picture) was part of the Borough of Bebington, the ferry buildings and pier were just inside the southern limit of the County Borough of Birkenhead. The New Ferry service was ailing when the pier was rammed by a coaster in fog in 1922 and dismantled, although the Rock Ferry service

continued. The ferry tollhouse survived as a residence till about 1960.

In this 1931 view the large apartment house with the square tower (centre) was the New Ferry Hotel in the heyday of the ferry; built in 1896-98, it replaced an older ferry hotel. The terrace of houses on the left has a private esplanade on the riverside. Brunel's ill-fated 690-foot-long steamship *Great Eastern* of 1857-59 ended its days on New Ferry shore, where it was broken up in 1888-90. It took two years to dismantle this huge vessel and fittings were auctioned locally. Some of these fittings can be seen behind the bar of the Great Eastern Hotel in New Ferry Road – carved and turned woodwork and frosted glass panels with a painted glass roundel of the great ship. *Valentine's postcard*

Top right Hazy sunlight breaks through the cloud and dances on the wide waters of the Mersey estuary at high tide as children and a dog play on **THE BEACH, NEW FERRY** in 1954. The trees of Rock Park, an early Victorian residential park, slope down to the esplanade, a rough track with a red sandstone retaining wall, which was a pleasant riverside walk from New Ferry to Rock Ferry. In the background Rock Ferry Pier stretches across the horizon, and beyond it we see (from left to right) the cranes of Cammell, Laird's shipbuilding yards at Tranmere, the Woodside ventilation shaft of the Mersey road tunnel, the three chimneys of Clarence Dock Power Station in Liverpool, the twin towers of the black Royal Liver Building, and shipping on the river. Rock Park was developed with villas for Liverpool professionals, ship-owners and merchants, who travelled across the river by Rock Ferry. Nathaniel Hawthorne, the American novelist and author of *Tanglewood Tales*, lived at 26 Rock Park from 1853 to 1857, when he was the American Consul in Liverpool.
In the 1950s Rock Park was still a private estate with tolls charged for visitors: 1d for a pedestrian, 2d for a bicycle and 6d for a car. This view was taken from the abutment for New Ferry Pier.

Above right 'Come to Rock Ferry for your holidays.' Here we see **ROCK FERRY PIER**, a small patch of sandy beach and a smart hotel. This was one of the first places in Wirral settled by wealthy Liverpool merchants and professional gentlemen escaping from the bustle and slums of the city across the river, commuting by the new steam ferries in the 1820s and '30s. Rock Ferry became something of a riverside resort in Edwardian times after the opening of the pier, but by the mid-20th century its fashionable past had been forgotten. There had been a ferry from 'The Rock' since the 17th century, plying to the south shore of Liverpool. The red sandstone slipway was built in 1820; 912 feet long with a paved runway for horse-drawn vehicles using the ferry, it also shipped cattle and handcarts. The first steam ferry called here in 1832.

Rock Park was developed by the Royal Rock Ferry Company from 1836 to 1850. The Royal Rock Hotel was a coach terminus with stables and 'pleasure gardens' and a meeting place of the Royal Rock Beagles of Bebington from their formation in 1846 till urbanisation drove the hounds out to Ledsham in 1925 (they are now in Flintshire). From the opening of the Birkenhead Railway in 1840, the ferry service became intermittent and was closed for periods as it passed through a succession of owners. Birkenhead Corporation took it over in 1897 and built the iron pier, which opened in 1899; it was 780 feet long with a hinged bridge to a floating landing stage, from which this 1952 view was taken. The end of the slipway was demolished to make way for the pier landing stage.

On the river frontage we see the Royal Rock Hotel, the single-storey Doric pavilion-style bath-house of 1836 and the trees of Rock Park. The stuccoed bath-house, for the use of sailors, was converted in about 1896 to Bath Cottages, which were still in occupation in the 1950s. The old ferry slipway is still used by fishermen and members of the Royal Mersey Yacht Club and Tranmere Sailing Club to get to their fishing-boats and yachts moored in the river off Rock Ferry and for landing fish.

COUNTY BOROUGH OF BIRKENHEAD
ROCK FERRY.
LANDING or EMBARKING
ONE PERSON } 1d
AT OWN RISK.
Issued subject to the Ferries Bye-Laws Rules
& Regulations, Vide Notices. Available day of
Issue only. Not Transferable.

Above The ferry service from Rock Ferry to Liverpool ended in 1939, but the pier stayed open till 1957 and you could still buy a ticket (*inset*) from the tollbooth inside the shabby, semi-derelict **ROCK FERRY PIER TOLLHOUSE** to walk along the half-ruined pier. In 1954 two people are walking towards the doorway under the left-hand bay of the three-bay iron colonnade supporting a glazed canopy. There was a matching colonnade on the other side of the building. All Mersey ferry passengers paid when landing or embarking on the Cheshire bank of the river. Here in ferry days passengers to Liverpool entered the right-hand side of the tollhouse and passengers from Liverpool paid at the left-hand ticket gates. On the gable below the clock tower was a white dial that showed the departure time of the next ferry to Liverpool.

The pier tollhouse stood at the foot of Rock Lane East and Bedford Road. The forecourt was originally half-enclosed by Victorian shops on the left, or north, side; of these, only the white building survived in the 1950s as a tea-room and sweet shop. The black shed behind it was a boathouse for 18-footers of the Royal Mersey Yacht Club, and the shed to the left of it

was the Tranmere Sailing Club house. In the 1920s and '30s the forecourt was a bus terminus. Birkenhead Corporation's first motor buses ran to Rock Ferry Pier in 1919, from Park station and from Moreton Cross. Corporation buses also ran from here to Woodhey from 1920 and to Port Sunlight from 1921. From 1924 six bus routes terminated here, with Crosville buses plying to Heswall via Storeton and to Raby Mere. These connections failed to save the losses on the ferry services and all passenger activity here ceased in 1939. The gas lamp post in the middle of the road survived the bus station but lost one of its brackets.

Below Fifty years earlier, the **ROCK FERRY PIER APPROACH**, viewed here from Bedford Road in 1904, was half-enclosed on the north side by the small Victorian shops. The lamp post in the middle of the road survived till our 1954 view, while the Rock Ferry Refreshment Room on the left-hand corner of Bedford Road survives today as a tavern. This postcard was mailed in 1908, franked 'Rock Ferry, Birkenhead', to an address in Everton. *Valentine's postcard*

Right You had to walk just over 300 yards along **ROCK FERRY PIER** out above the Mersey and down the sloping bridge to the floating landing stage to catch the ferry, with the Lancashire coast at Dingle just a mile ahead across the river. Like most Mersey ferry piers there were railings along the middle of the pier deck to divide the two-way flow of passengers, those landing at Rock Ferry walking on the left and those embarking for Liverpool on the right. After the ferry service finished in 1939 that half of the pier deck used by embarking passengers was closed to save maintenance costs, and the remainder was kept open for the use of fishermen, tugmen, yachtsmen and promenaders. This picture was taken by the glazed wooden shelter halfway along the pier in 1954; the next shelter

in the distance was at the end of the pier at the top of the sloping bridge. It was a precarious feeling walking down the bridge, especially when it sloped steeply at low water. The bridge was 160 feet long and only 10ft 6 in wide. Rock Ferry Pier was a location for boys' adventures in the 1950 Ealing film *The Magnet*, shot mainly in New Brighton and Liverpool.

Below The Birkenhead Corporation screw steamers *Storeton* and *Upton* ran a half-hourly service to Liverpool until closure in 1939. The service extended to New Ferry until that pier was wrecked in 1922. The double-ended paddle steamers of the Eastham company also called at Rock Ferry on the way from Liverpool to Eastham from 1901 to 1914; this service ended in 1929. In the 1950s **ROCK FERRY LANDING STAGE** was used by tugs and the dinghies of fishermen and yachtsmen, and in 1954 their boats are neatly ranged within the painted and numbered spaces allotted. The tug berthed here is a 'Cock' tug of the Liverpool Screw Towage & Lighterage Company. The old ferry fog bell and navigation light were still in place in the wooden tower on the edge of the stage. The store shed was the survivor of two similar arch-roofed wooden structures, one each side of the foot of the bridge, used as a passenger waiting room and a stagemen's shelter. The lean-to extension was added during the Second World War for some wartime use of the pier. The stage was quite small – 150 feet long and 45 feet wide – no bigger than one of the Mersey ferry steamers of the period 1930-60. In the background we can see smoke from a ship on the river (centre) and Liverpool waterfront (right).

Above Part of the pier tollhouse and the river can be seen between the trees at the end of **BEDFORD ROAD, ROCK FERRY**. The picture was taken in 1949 from the corner of Haddon Road (right) in the town centre shopping area around the crossing of Bedford Road and New Chester Road. This was the way the townspeople went on foot, bicycle and bus to the ferry to go to work in Liverpool in the 1920s and '30s. In the 1950s it was a quiet residential backwater leading to a pleasant walk along the pier or the Esplanade. The shops on the right were a greengrocer's, a printing works and a tobacconist's. At the end of the road on the left are the headquarters of the Royal Mersey Yacht Club, founded in 1844. *Valentine's postcard*

Below The substantial brick and stone booking hall of **ROCK FERRY STATION** on Bedford Road stood on top of the bridge over the main line from Chester to Birkenhead. The Birkenhead Joint Railway, owned by the London & North Western Railway (LNWR) and the GWR, opened a station

here in 1862, but these buildings date from the quadrupling of the tracks from Ledsham to Birkenhead in 1902-08. The booking hall on the bridge gave direct access down steps to all platforms and saved on land purchase.

Over the bridge Bedford Road sloped straight down through Rock Ferry town centre to the pier. Most of the shops lined New Chester Road north of Bedford Road crossing. In 1954 we see the familiar rounded shape of a blue, Massey-bodied Birkenhead Corporation bus as it pauses to load passengers outside the Bedford Hotel on route 42 from Overchurch to Bromborough via Charing Cross. Two soldiers in khaki battledress are carrying kitbags towards the bus. The Bedford Hotel dispensed Cornbrook Ales and was known as Luke Lee's, after a well-known licensee of the early 20th century. The newsvendor outside the station, with a home-made box on pram wheels, was Jack Kay, who lived behind the hotel in Lees Avenue (probably named after the licensee). He had this pitch from the Second World War till 1969, and sold the *Liverpool Echo* and the *Evening Express* – 'Echo … Express!' was a familiar street cry on Merseyside. On winter evenings his gloom was lit by the gas lamp on the ornate iron bracket over the station doorway.

Below These pioneer, American-style, wooden **MERSEY RAILWAY** electric trains lured passengers off Woodside-bound steam trains at Rock Ferry station and droned through the brick-lined, double-track tunnels to cavernous, dimly lit underground stations with tiled walls and newsagents' and tobacconists' kiosks on the platforms in central Birkenhead and Liverpool. This was the southern terminus of the Mersey Railway's 5-mile system built in 1886-92 as a steam railway to Liverpool Central and Birkenhead Park. Despite condensing

apparatus on the locomotives, the acrid atmosphere in the 4 miles of tunnel, with gradients of 1 in 27 and 1 in 30 under the river, made this the first steam railway in Britain to be electrified. The American firm Westinghouse did the job – with no interruption of steam service – in 1901-03, shipping all its electrical equipment and running gear from Pennsylvania. The company power station in Shore Road, Birkenhead, fed 650 volts dc through a side conductor rail, while the centre rail returned current to the power station. Car sheds and workshops were at Birkenhead Central.

Here in 1954 is one of the original multiple unit train sets of 1903 with coachwork by George Milnes, who had moved his workshops from Birkenhead to Hadley, Shropshire, in 1900-02. Under the Westinghouse contract they were built to the contemporary American design with clerestory roofs and matchboard panels. These old trains worked through to New Brighton after the 1938 electrification of north Wirral lines by the London Midland & Scottish Railway (LMS), and had their earth-lead adapted to switch over to the three-rail system beyond Birkenhead Park.

The Mersey Railway remained independent until nationalised in 1948. Its dark Indian-red trains were repainted between 1950 and 1954 in the malachite green of British Railways multiple-unit stock. The 3rd Class return fare from Rock Ferry to Liverpool Central in 1953 was 1 shilling. The centre rails were removed in 1956 after the running rails were bonded for the return current for use by ex-LMS and BR three-rail electric trains, and these old Mersey Railway electrics were retired from service in 1956-57. Rock Ferry station had six platforms – four on the main line and two on the Mersey Railway – spanned by a covered wooden footbridge with four wooden lift towers.

Above   At the bottom of St Paul's Road in **SOUTH TRANMERE** was a graveyard of old coasters and barges on the Mersey shore. Many a vessel that was too decrepit to be insured for further service or had been crippled in collision in the busy Mersey estuary ended up on this stretch of shore south of Tranmere shipbuilding yards. These were the remains of the shipbreakers Victor Sellers and previously Kaye & Dennit. In 1954 a cloth-capped labourer takes time out to watch the ships go by on the river – this was the only point of public access to the riverside at Tranmere. We see a trail of white steam from the tall funnel of a dredger heading down-river. On the

Liverpool bank, a mile across the water, we can see the granaries of the Liverpool Grain Storage & Transit Company at Coburg Dock and, a mile beyond, the tower of Liverpool Cathedral. St Paul's Road, which leads down to the shore here, was previously Lime Kiln Lane and had a station of that name on the Birkenhead & Chester Railway from 1846; renamed Tranmere in 1853, it closed in 1857.

Below   Sporting the garter coat of arms of the Birkenhead Brewery Company in the panel formed by the dummy window, the dingy little **MERSEY INN, TRANMERE** stood on the

corner of Croxteth Street at 246 New Chester Road in Lower Tranmere. Photographed in 1954, Croxteth Street (left) was one of a small grid of short back streets sandwiched between the railway viaduct and the hurly-burly of the New Chester Road (right) at the approaches to Birkenhead. Next was Clare Street, casting its shaft of light across the main road, and then we can see the rusticated cornerstones of the Lord Raglan public house on the corner of Union Street.

Above right   **NEW CHESTER ROAD, TRANMERE**, formed part of the A41 trunk road from London and Chester, and approached Birkenhead through a stretch of drab, industrial no-man's-land in Lower Tranmere with pungent smells from the British Leather Company's

tannery and Thomson Brothers' glue factory. They were supplied by the Birkenhead Corporation slaughterhouse (right) on this bend by Cammell, Laird's shipyard gates (to the right of the Belisha beacons). The Royal Castle Hotel to the left of the beacons took its name from the former Royal Mail coach terminus here and the castellated ferry buildings at the entrance to the former Tranmere Pier on the Mersey bank at this point. The hotel stands at the corner of Green Lane (left), which brought the old Chester coach road down to the ferry; in 1833 the New Chester Road was built straight from Bromborough to Lower Tranmere by Thomas Brassey, and the old and new roads converged here by the hotel.

Tranmere had a ferry service to Liverpool at least from the 16th century and a pioneer steam ferry from 1817. The stone pier and slipway and the iron pier of 1877 extended into the river where the fitting-out basin of the shipyard is today. Tranmere Ferry closed in 1904 and the Birkenhead shipyards were extended south to cover a total of 108 acres along 1,033 yards of the Cheshire bank south of Monks Ferry. In 1954 the Leyland Octopus four-axle flatbed lorry with a trailer is passing the gables of the slaughterhouse. The lamp post on the left is a former tramway traction pole; an ornate bracket (a bit lower down the pole than the plain lamp bracket here)

reached out to the middle of the road to support the electric wires on the New Ferry line, which closed in 1931.

Below An advertisement for Cammell, Laird's shipyard, Tranmere, from the 1951 *Birkenhead Official Guide*, showing the second *Mauretania* for the Cunard White Star Line. At 771 feet and 35,677 gross tons, this ten-deck liner was not only the largest ship then built at Birkenhead but also the largest from an English yard in her time, the 'Queens' being Clyde-built. More than 7,000 men were employed in her construction, she was launched in 1938 and made her maiden voyage from Liverpool in 1939. She had luxurious accommodation for 1,337 passengers, three cinemas, cargo capacity for 12,050 tons, and a service speed of 23 knots. She was a troopship during the Second World War and on return to passenger service after the war made record passages to Singapore. From 1947 she plied the Cunard route between Southampton, Le Havre and New York with the famous 'Queen' liners, and cruised to the Mediterranean and the West Indies. She had a crew of 593, mostly from Merseyside, and always revisited the Mersey for a refit. She last visited the river in 1963 for her annual overhaul in Gladstone dry dock, then in 1965 she was withdrawn from service and broken up at Inverkeithing.

CAMMELL LAIRD & CO. LTD.

BIRKENHEAD

Cunard White Star Passenger Liner "Mauretania"

SHIPBUILDERS

ENGINEERS

REPAIRERS

BOILERMAKERS

MERCHANT AND WAR VESSELS	SEVEN GRAVING DOCKS
OF ALL TYPES. ENGINES AND	RANGING UP TO 880 FEET IN
BOILERS. GEARED TURBINES.	LENGTH, AND A FITTING-OUT
OIL ENGINES. BUILDING SLIPS	BASIN OF 14 ACRES. CRANES
RANGING UP TO 1000 FEET.	UP TO 200 TONS CAPACITY

Above **OLD CHESTER ROAD, TRANMERE** converges from the left in this view along Queen Street. It runs from Lower Tranmere to Lower Bebington and was part of the old coach road from Woodside ferry to Chester from 1790 (when a causeway was built across Tranmere Pool) till the opening of the New Chester Road in 1833. Between 1816 and 1866 coaches also ran through Old Chester Road between Tranmere Ferry and Parkgate to connect with ferries across the Dee to Bagillt and Flint; this was one way that people travelled between Liverpool and north Wales.

The triangle formed by Old Chester Road, Queen Street and Green Lane was the former village of Hinderton (hence the name Hinderton Road leading from Argyle Street South to Queen Street), but with urbanisation from about 1860 this district became known as Lower Tranmere. The original village of Tranmere was on top of the hill on the older ridgeway coach road to Woodside (before 1790), now Church Road, Higher

Tranmere. Before the development of Birkenhead in the 1820s Tranmere was the largest settlement in north Wirral. It was incorporated into the new Borough of Birkenhead in 1877, but the Corporation declined to take over the ferry, which remained independent and intermittent till closure in 1904. Green Lane was the southern terminus of the Mersey Railway from 1886 till the extension to Rock Ferry in 1891.

The white building on the left of this 1954 picture is the Harp Inn, dating from the late 18th century. Beyond it the street of shabby houses and shops narrows to the Birkenhead & District Co-op shop on the corner of Albert Place, followed by three pawnbrokers' shops. In the shadows on the right is W. Turner's grocery shop at 50 Queen Street; an archway beyond it leads to Stewart Place. Behind the houses on the right tower the 40-foot cliffs of the disused Hinderton Quarry, which provided the stone for building much of 19th-century Birkenhead.

Left The 1954 photograph of the scene more closely resembles this painting by William Herdman done 86 years earlier than the same location today. Herdman was a Liverpool painter who spent much time on location on the Cheshire bank in the 1860s and seemed particularly attracted to the rustic old township of Tranmere, which pre-dated Birkenhead. Many of his paintings of the riverside townships and ferry landing places from Tranmere to New Brighton are to be found in the local collection at Birkenhead art gallery. *Williamson Art Gallery & Museum, Birkenhead*

Above right **MOLLINGTON STREET, TRANMERE**, a dead-end back street off Argyle Street South, was the access to Birkenhead railway loco sheds, which stabled a large stud of ex-GWR, LNWR and LMS locomotives. The shed roofs with their smoke cowls are seen on the left beyond the houses, with the cranes of Tranmere shipyards in the background. There were coal sidings behind the houses on the right and the Mersey Railway ran under the bridge halfway along the street between Birkenhead Central station and the tunnel to Green Lane; the

bridge also spanned a link line between Central and the loco sheds. Thus the 13 houses beyond the bridge were on an island surrounded by railways. Mollington Street had a blacksmith's workshop and a total of 19 houses, which were home (in 1954) to an locomotive cleaner, a boiler-maker, a clerk, a painter, a stevedore and several labourers and their families. The houses on the left backed on to Birkenhead gasworks. By night the street was dimly lit by three gas lanterns.

Right New Chester Road gave way to **CHESTER STREET** as the A41 trunk road passed under this railway bridge, which formed the 'gateway to Birkenhead'. Advertising Ferodo brake linings, it carried tracks leading to Abbey Street coal sidings and Cammell, Laird's shipbuilding yards and dry docks. Chester Street slopes up from the level of Tranmere Pool on to the headland on which Birkenhead was built. The two public houses on the left, at the corner of Waterloo Place, were the Shakespeare Hotel and the Prince Alfred. At the top of the slope the gap on the left side of the street, marked by the blank gable wall, was King's Square, entrance to the Mersey road tunnel. The clock tower of Birkenhead Town Hall can be seen in the distance. The dark blue Bedford

furniture van descending Chester Street in 1954 is one of the fleet of Wright Brothers, furniture removers, of 16 New Chester Road, New Ferry. The main railway line from London and Chester, which gradually converged with the New Chester Road from the left-hand side, went underground at the disused Birkenhead Town station on Grange Street and tunnelled under King's Square and Chester Street to emerge on the right-hand side of the street at Woodside terminus by the ferry.

Above Two blocks of the old Birkenhead town centre, including the central library, shops and slums north of the corner of Chester Street and Market Place South, were cleared in the early 1930s to make way for the impressive **MERSEY TUNNEL ENTRANCE**. The tunnel under the river was opened in 1934 by King George V and Queen Mary, who went on to open a new central library the same day – the tunnel was named Queensway and the entrance King's Square. Herbert Rowse was the architect of the four tunnel entrances and six ventilation stations on both sides of the river. The Portland stone portal, retaining walls and the flanking triumphal arches in the restrained neo-classical style of the 1930s were an incongruous splash of white in the otherwise soot-black townscape of Birkenhead, as was the new Portland stone library in its context of Borough Road.

The long Market Hall (1843-45) runs behind the left-hand arch and retaining wall. On the right-hand side, above the tunnel mouth, is a four-storey, grimy, stone post-Georgian terrace fronting Cross Street, the surviving half of the Market Cross shopping centre of 1847. It is a triangular terrace, fronting Chester Street, Market Street and Cross Street. The matching triangular other half of Market Cross, fronting Cross Street, Monk Street and Albion Street, was demolished for the tunnel. The clock tower of Birkenhead Town Hall is prominent among the buildings behind the portal.

The massive, fluted, black granite lighting column on the right is a monument to the building of the Mersey Tunnel in 1926-34. Its base is inscribed with the names of the committee, engineers and contractors for the building of the tunnel, which was promoted, funded and administered by the Mersey Tunnel Joint Committee of Liverpool and Birkenhead Corporations. This 60-foot column stood on an island of gardens dividing the motor traffic entering the leaving the tunnel. Four green wooden tollbooths, looking like short tramcar bodies, sold tickets at each end of the tunnel.

Three 'spivvy' cars of the 1950s are just leaving the tollbooths to enter the tunnel in this 1961 view; they are (from the left) a 1958 Messerschmitt two-seater aircraft cockpit on three wheels, a 1956 American-designed Austin-Nash Metropolitan, and a 1959 Austin Cambridge/Morris Oxford. Two railway tunnels run under King's Square, diverging to Monks Ferry and Woodside.

Below left From King's Square the **MERSEY TUNNEL** curves left to cross the Mersey Railway tunnel and pass under Hamilton Square, then curves right below Pacific Road. It then burrows beneath the river bed in a straight line from Woodside ventilation shaft to Brunswick Street, Liverpool, between the Cunard and Dock Buildings. The junction seen here, under the corner of Bridge Street and Sandford Street, Birkenhead, is where the four-lane main tunnel, approaching from Liverpool, curves left towards King's Square and the two-lane dock branch tunnel forks off to the right to the Rendel Street entrance. There was also a dock branch tunnel in Liverpool, and the two junctions were controlled by signals. In peak periods the Birkenhead branch exit and the Liverpool branch entrance were closed so that there was no traffic conflict at these junctions, but you could still enter the Birkenhead branch and leave by the Liverpool branch. Including the ramps required to cross under three-quarters of a mile of river, the tunnel is 2 miles long from King's Square, Birkenhead, to Old Haymarket, Liverpool, and nearly 3 miles with the two dock branches.

The tunnel was built in 1926-34 to relieve traffic congestion on the vehicular ferries and unemployment in the Depression. It was dug out from each side of the river through solid sandstone bedrock with gelignite and pneumatic drills, and 1,200,000 tons of rock were shifted to land reclamation sites at Storeton quarry, Dingle and Otterspool. The steel and concrete archway was plastered and painted off-white to simulate Portland stone, with recessed lights and a black glass dado. The roadway is 36 feet wide in the main tunnel and 19 feet wide in the branch tunnels. On the left is a Tunnel Police van, a navy blue Fordson of 1946, and on the right a 1937 Morris 10 car. Six ventilation stations keep the air clean in the tunnel, the three in Birkenhead being Woodside, Sidney Street and Taylor Street. *Tokim postcard*

Below The north end of **CHESTER STREET**, Birkenhead, was the final stretch of the A41 route from London and the old coach route from Chester to Woodside. In 1954 we are looking north from the corner of Pilgrim Street (right) with the doorway and lantern of the Clarendon Hotel on the near corner. Lloyd's printing works was on the opposite corner; the fine, curved, ashlar stone facade above it was defaced with advertising hoardings. On the left-hand side of the street the National Assistance Board office occupied a former public house that had originally been the Birkenhead Assembly Rooms on the corner of Market Street. The next gap on the left is Duncan Street. Willmer Brothers' *Birkenhead News* office and printing works occupied the block to Brandon Street. Then we see the facade of the Sessions House (1884-87), which backs on to the Town Hall. The view is terminated by the 210-foot Woodside ventilation shaft of the Mersey road tunnel standing on the river bank (1934). All six lamp posts in this picture are former Birkenhead Corporation tramway traction poles, complete with the original bracket arms with ornamental scrollwork. The last tramcars ran along Chester Street to New Ferry in 1931 and the Birkenhead system closed down progressively till the last cars ran to Oxton and Claughton in 1937. Running underneath this stretch of Chester Street is the railway tunnel to Woodside.

Below Still in 1954 we are looking south along **CHESTER STREET** from the corner of Bridge Street, with the Queen's Arms Hotel of 1840 on the right and a 1935 Austin motor car parked opposite. The 1940 Crosville bus, with its ugly, protruding destination box, is standing on Church Street bridge over the railway cutting at the approach to Woodside station. The railway emerges from Chester Street tunnel under the black gable wall of the first houses on the left in Chester Street. Clouds of steam and smoke and the noise of gruff, barking exhaust and squealing flanges often erupted over the stepped and stone-capped brick wall as trains started out of the terminus up the 1 in 95 gradient of the curving tunnel.

The two terraced blocks of houses ending in blank gable walls above the tunnel mouth were originally one V-plan terrace, built about 1830, in the fork of Chester Street and Church Street, forming, together with the Queen's Arms, an impressive classical entrance to Chester Street on the crest of the slope up from the ferry. These buildings stood alone for several years in the piecemeal development of the town, and the terrace was cut in two at its vertex by the railway extension to Woodside in the 1870s. Church Street led to Birkenhead Priory Church of St Mary, which was the parish church of Birkenhead from 1821 to 1970. The street also led to Monks Ferry coaling station for tugs, and Cammell, Laird's dry docks. Between Monks Ferry Brow and St Mary's Church was a no-go area of gaunt, brick slum tenements, where the streets were littered with broken glass.

Bottom These Regency houses in Chester Street were some of the oldest houses of nascent Birkenhead, built about 1830 at the end of the Regency period with such characteristics as the flights of steps with railings up to the main floors above basements and the front doors framed by Tuscan pillars and semi-circular fanlights and brick arches. They were built in traditional Cheshire, dusky, red-brown, brindled brickwork, further variegated here by yellow brick headers to give a chequered appearance. The last three houses at the right-hand end of the terrace are sheathed in stucco, more typical of Regency buildings.

These houses, numbered 37 to 53 Chester Street, were originally the homes of Liverpool ship-owners, merchants and artisans, the first settlers of Birkenhead. No 49, the first of the stuccoed houses, was at one time the Golden Lion public house. The railway was extended to Woodside in a tunnel underneath this terrace in 1878, and the houses to the left of No 37 were demolished, the smoke-blackened gable wall towering above the tunnel mouth where trains blasted upgrade out of Woodside on their way to Chester. By the 1950s these houses had fallen on hard times. Nos 37 to 47 were the homes of labourers, stevedores and railwaymen, and the last three houses had been converted: the former Golden Lion was now The Abbey Canteen Dining Rooms and the shop front with twin pediments at the end of the terrace formed the workshop of J. Banks & Sons, ships' block-makers, and later Seaman & Winstanley, precision engineers. This photograph was taken in 1974.

Above right Chester Street slopes down the river bank towards Woodside Ferry between the Woodside Hotel (right) and the train shed of Woodside station (left). Crosville country buses wait to load passengers up the slope and an incoming Crosville bus stops to unload outside the Queen's Arms Hotel at the corner of Bridge Street. The Woodside Hotel was built in 1833-34 on the river bank and was a busy coaching inn at the top of the ferry slipway before the reclamation of the present ferry approach and the coming of the railway. It stands on the site of an earlier ferry inn where stormbound passengers lodged and from which the first regular coach service plied to Chester in 1762. The single-storey annexe behind the hotel was the Crosville bus office for inspectors, inquiries and parcels. There are three inns up the right-hand side of the slope in this 1954 picture: the Woodside Hotel, the Woodside Vaults right behind

it (with a cul-de-sac in between) and the Queen's Arms. The silhouette of the County Sessions House stands on the skyline of Chester Street, and the clock tower of the Town Hall peeps over the roof of the Woodside Vaults.

Below **WOODSIDE** was the great terminus on the Mersey bank. Ferries have plied across the river from Woodside to Liverpool since the 13th century, stage services have come to meet the ferries since 1762, and the Great Western Railway main line from Paddington was diverted from Monks Ferry to Woodside Ferry in 1878. Beside the great twin-arch train shed (right) is the busy bus station. Crosville's green country buses stand on the north slope of Chester Street loading for Loggerheads, Chester and Heswall, while another departs for Ellesmere Port. This Chester company, founded in 1911, covered Cheshire, north and mid-Wales and the southern tip of Lancashire between Warrington and Liverpool. Beyond are blue Birkenhead Corporation buses occupying the bus station and storage road at the approach to Woodside Ferry tollhouse.

On the left of the bus station are the black gabled cattle sheds of the Mersey Cattle Wharf.

In 1954, from the top of the slope, on the corner of Bridge Street (left), we can see the three-quarter-mile passage of the Woodside Ferry across the Mersey to Liverpool waterfront, with its impressive trio of office buildings on George's Pier Head: the lordly black Royal Liver Building with twin clock towers fore and aft, which dominated the Merseyside scene, the squat Cunard Building, and the domed Dock Office. These three buildings were erected in 1907-16 as a fitting frontage to the great ocean terminus, and they make a stirring backdrop to views across the river from Birkenhead and for the ferries that ply from Woodside and Seacombe. In the left foreground is the rear portal of the Mersey Motor Company works, which fronted on to Hamilton Street. The long pedestrian crossing, previously shown only by the Belisha beacons and studs, has been marked out with the more striking white bands of a 'zebra' crossing, first painted on British streets in 1951. The de-rationing of petrol in 1950 led to a post-war motoring boom.

Above **WOODSIDE STATION** was the northernmost railhead of the legendary Great Western empire on the Mersey bank. The GWR shared this terminus with the LNWR – which after 1923 became part of the LMS – for joint operations to Chester and the Helsby and West Kirby branches via Hooton. The GWR ran the trunk line services from here to Shrewsbury, Birmingham and London (Paddington), to Llangollen, Barmouth and Pwllheli, to Reading, Southampton and Bournemouth, and to Guildford, Ashford and Margate, bringing Southern Railway carriages to Woodside as well. Through carriages on these trains went on to Cardiff, Paignton, Penzance, Brighton, Eastbourne, Hastings, Folkestone, Dover and Sandwich.

In 1959 a Paddington train is drawn up in platform 1 (right); there were six up and six down trains a day on this route for most of the 1950s, when the great train shed echoed to a total of 90 arrivals and departures a day and the almost constant loading and unloading of parcels and mailbags. The exhaust of steam locomotives starting trains up the 1 in 95 gradient through Chester Street tunnel echoed off the stone-walled cutting, the bridges and the buildings around. The twin-arched, glazed, cast-iron curved roof spanned five short, wide platforms, with a motor road for luggage vans between platforms 1 and 2.

The platforms could accommodate only eight-coach trains because space was short between the tunnel mouth and the river wall. The station roof was also short, to allow a street, Rose Brae, to bridge the platforms in a long iron trough; this was a cul-de-sac leading to the Grayson, Rollo & Clover dry docks south of the station. The white cliff of the Queen's Arms Hotel and the black clock tower of Birkenhead Town Hall are framed in the northern arch of the train shed.

Woodside station was built in 1878; the former terminus at Monks Ferry (1844) remained in use by the Monks Ferry Steam Coal Company to bunker Mersey tugs and coasters. The original Birkenhead railway terminus had opened at Grange Lane in 1840.

Below Rose Brae led off the north slope of Chester Street to the back of Woodside station and the adjacent six dry docks of Grayson, Rollo & Clover along the river bank south of the station. The superstructure of a ship in the north-end dry dock can be seen above the stone wall (left). When the dock was full and the ship afloat, the superstructure towered high above trains entering Woodside station. The ornate cast-iron portico seen here in 1954, used as a loading bay for parcels vans, and the Victorian Gothic station booking hall and offices behind it

were designed as the frontage of the railway terminus, but the station was built the wrong way round relative to the ferry entrance and the tram terminus. Thus passengers did not use this entrance, and the arcaded, windowless back wall of the train shed faced the ferry approach. The line-up of railway company motor vehicles berthed for loading under the portico comprises an Austin lorry, a Dennis van, two Karrier vans and another Austin, all built in the 1940s. The clock tower of Birkenhead Town Hall once more dominates the skyline.

This 1924 photograph is an enlargement from a postcard by the same publisher as the 1951 view on the next page. It shows the **WOODSIDE FERRY TRAM TERMINUS** from the same viewpoint less than 30 years earlier, with a line-up of tramcars on the track-fan of six sidings in front of the ferry tollhouse looking like the start of the great tram race! A single traction pole in the middle of the road carries an expansive bracket arm suspending the overhead wires for all six sidings, and at the far end the wires are rigged to three poles protruding through the canopy of the ferry tollhouse. The foreshortening of the view obscures the fact that there are, from right to left, two cars on each of the roads 1, 2 and 4, and one car on each of the roads 3 and 5, making a total of eight tramcars in the picture, although there was room here for 22; road 6 is vacant. From left to right we can see cars on lines D (Docks), C (Circle via Conway Street) and T (Tranmere), and spare cars in the afternoon off-peak period parked on the two right-hand sidings, allocated to New Ferry cars.

The cars were painted cream and maroon and the wooden saloons were decorated with carved window pillars and doorways with the Borough motto cut into carved scrollwork over the sliding doors and ornate patterns in transfers on the ceilings. Three cars have clerestory roofs, unusual on double-deckers, and three have semi-elliptical arched roofs, which were a characteristic feature of both Birkenhead and Wallasey trams. Birkenhead replaced its tramcars with motor buses over the period from 1925 to 1937. The upright funnel of one of the double-ended goods ferry steamers is seen at the landing stage at the end of the floating road. *Valentine's postcard*

The A41 road from London terminated here alongside the GWR from London (right), and all roads into Birkenhead funnel into the **WOODSIDE FERRY APPROACH,** which was also the focal point of the Birkenhead Corporation bus system. Off-peak service buses took their terminal lay-over time at the sheltered stands, peak-period buses were stored in the spare bus rank on the left to save dead mileage to and from the depot, and private cars were allowed to park in a single line astern along the middle of the bus station. The grey (formerly red) sandstone pavilions on the left, fronting the spare bus rank, were built about 1870 as railway inquiry and parcels offices (GWR on the left, LNWR on the right) when the railway terminus was at Monks Ferry, and they were later converted to public lavatories (gentlemen on the left, ladies on the right). A notice board on the ladies points cyclists going by ferry to use the floating road, entered to the left of the gents. The floating road ran on pontoons down the defile between the spare bus rank and the black sheds of the cattle lairage.

This 1951 photograph was taken from the Woodside Hotel, providing a dramatic view over the bus station and the ferry tollhouse across the Mersey to Liverpool waterfront, with the barrack-like Albert Dock warehouses (1845) on the right and the Liver, Cunard and Dock Buildings on the left, appropriately fronted by a Cunard liner moored in mid-river at low water. It is a windy day with white horses on the river, the Union flag on the ferry tollhouse outstretched, and the air on the ebb tide filled with a strong admixture of the refreshing smells of fresh water and salt water. *Valentine's postcard*

Above Birkenhead Corporation buses – Daimlers, Leylands and a Guy, all with Massey bodies – wait at the loading platforms on the ferry approach at **WOODSIDE BUS STATION** during a quiet mid-morning period in 1951. Older wartime Guys and pre-war Leylands, reserved for peak periods, are parked on the storage road on the left, behind the sandstone lavatory block on the corner. The few ferry commuters who came by private car were allowed to park along the middle of the bus station, where we see a 1936 Jaguar, a 1949 Austin Hampshire A70, a 1935 Morris 8, another Jaguar and a Rover. (Most car owners drove through the Mersey Tunnel.)

The ferry terminus and the entire area in this view were developed in 1858-66 on reclaimed land as part of a new river wall from Woodside to Seacombe, with dock entrances. A short lighthouse on the river wall to the left of the tollhouse once stood at the head of the former stone pier of 1835, which jutted out from the natural river bank at the foot of the slope below the Woodside Hotel, from which this photograph was taken; the old pier is embedded beneath the bus storage road.

The bus station was enclosed in the angle between the ferry tollhouse, which terminates this view, and the arcaded brick wall of Woodside station train shed on the right. The arch that served as the main station entrance for passengers, taxicabs and vans can be seen between the two buses on the right, marked by a V-shaped twin signboard projecting above the arch, reading 'Birkenhead Woodside Station' – although the architects designed this as the back of the station, not the front. The legend 'London Midland Scottish and Great Western Joint Railways Woodside Station' was painted in large fading white capitals on flaking black paintwork along the brick parapet – and again across the twin arches facing the Mersey. The brick and stone building with chimneys between the ferry tollhouse and the station housed Woodside Post Office and Crosville Motor Services' inquiries and parcels office on the ground floor and the British School of Motoring upstairs. The Birkenhead Corporation bus inquiries, lost property and inspectors' office was at the left-hand end of the ferry building.

Above Parked at Woodside bus station in 1954 is one of the 40 Leyland Titan TD5Cs with bodies by Massey Brothers of Pemberton, Wigan. Built in 1939, they set a style for Massey-bodied buses delivered to Birkenhead over the next 19 years (with the exception of the angular wartime utility design), and this style of bus, with slight modifications in later batches, was

seen on the streets of Birkenhead until 1975. These pre-war buses were like cartoon caricatures, with their well-rounded roof domes and windows, the semi-circular ends of the lower saloon windows, the flared skirting of the side and back panels and the curved body flange to the front nearside mudguard, all features of 1930s modern styling. They were usually to be seen with their bonnet side panels leaning open and rattling, maybe to help cool the engines, which blurted out a guttural belching noise.

The 'C' suffix of TD5C indicated that the bus was built with a hydraulic torque converter; it had the words 'Gearless Bus' on the radiator. This was standard for all Birkenhead buses built from 1933 to 1939 for the ease of former tramcar motormen not used to changing gear. The 1939 batch was converted to manual gear change by 1950. This bus is in the 1945 to 1950 paint scheme, with the standard blue livery extended along the length of the roof and the lower saloon windows. Upper saloon ceilings were ribbed with exposed arched beams that were part of the wood frame of the body. These 1939 buses were retired from service in 1955-57, No 311 going in 1956. North Circle route 90 ran via Argyle Street, Claughton Road, Tollemache Road, Beaufort Road and Cleveland Street back to Woodside. The vehicles on the left are a 1953 Austin A35, a 1932 Morris Minor two-seater sports coupé and a wartime Crosville bus.

Right Also at **WOODSIDE BUS STATION** in 1954 is a 1949 Birkenhead Guy. With the same rounded and flared body as the pre-war design, stout corner window pillars and panelled ceiling upstairs, the post-war Birkenhead bus with a Massey body on a Guy or Daimler chassis looked an altogether more noble beast and sounded like it too, with the deep-throated throb and gear whine of the six-cylinder Gardner diesel engine. This was one of a batch of 15 Guy Arabs that served Birkenhead from 1949 to 1962-63. A total of 85 Daimlers and Guys with this style of Massey bodywork (including 15 wartime Guys rebodied in 1953) operated in Birkenhead in the 1950s and '60s, the last nine, built in 1956, retiring from service in 1972.

No 147, seen here, is in the post-1950 livery with cream lower windows. Like

all Birkenhead buses of the period, it had blue leather seats and chrome handrails. It is loading alongside Woodside railway station for the New Chester Road route to Rock Ferry, New Ferry and Bromborough. Fares from Woodside in 1953 were 4d to Port Sunlight, 5d to Bromborough Cross, and 7d to Manor Road terminus. The fares were collected by a peripatetic conductor and placed in a leather shoulder-bag, and he issued tickets like those shown here from a wooden ticket rack he carried in his hand. Birkenhead Corporation bus routes extended well beyond the borough boundary, and the blue and cream livery was seen as far afield as Eastham, Clatterbridge, Heswall, Thurstaston, Moreton shore and New Brighton. The car facing us on the left is a Wolseley 450, also of 1949.

Bottom left Buses on 'siesta time' stand casually in the wide open space outside **BIRKENHEAD CENTRAL STATION** in 1954, while a couple with a child stroll across the road on the long pedestrian crossing, marked only by studs. The buses are standing in a triangle formed by three streets. Argyle Street South shafts across the picture from the foreground up the hill to Higher Tranmere. The building on the left is St Paul's School in Wilbraham Street, which has buildings on one side only. Borough Road crosses the scene from left to right in front of the station. The King Edward VII memorial clock tower (1912) once stood in gardens in the middle of this triangle. The two Birkenhead buses and the Wallasey bus parked here on short-workings to Central station are continuing the tradition of the former tramway loop here around the clock tower, which was moved across the square in 1929 to a larger triangle of gardens bounded by Argyle Street South, Borough Road and Clifton Crescent, off to the right of the picture. The policeman (extreme right) is standing on the corner of Clifton Crescent.

The lamp posts in the picture are former tramway traction poles, which held up the cobweb of span wires for the overhead running wires. The kiosk, like a large telephone box on the island outside Central station, was a Birkenhead Corporation bus inspectors' kiosk in blue and cream. The long colonnade curving around the front of the station was a shelter for passengers waiting at the stops there for Corporation and Crosville buses. The lettering along the fascia of the colonnade reads: 'Birkenhead Corporation and Crosville bus stop'. Central station, dated 1886, was an 'alfresco' station on the underground Mersey Railway; accommodating company offices, with the line's car sheds and workshops alongside, it was in a cutting between two tunnels.

Below As the bus rolls into town along Cleveland Street, a sudden change of scene unfolds as the mean streets of dockland give way to the impressive grandeur of **HAMILTON SQUARE**. This is the view from Cleveland Street at the Argyle Street crossing, looking across the north side of the square towards Hamilton Street in the background, with the Town Hall on the right. This north-east corner of Hamilton Square was built first, in 1826, and stood in isolation until the west and south sides (Argyle Street and Price Street) were built from 1839 to 1844, while the east side (Hamilton Street) was not completed till 1844-46. The ivy-covered, grimy, stone-faced terraces are of five storeys, with three main floors, an attic above the cornice and a basement below the steps. In 1954 a blue Birkenhead bus (nearest the camera) is returning to Woodside Ferry on the Oxton Circle route 4, having turned right here from Argyle Street, while two yellow Wallasey buses are turning left into Hamilton Street, the hinder one showing route 10 from New Brighton to New Ferry.

Above From this corner of Hamilton Square, **HAMILTON STREET** slopes down the Mersey bank towards Woodside Ferry, and between the buildings we can just see the Royal Liver Building on Liverpool waterfront just over a mile away across the river. Prominent on the left-hand side of the street in this 1954 photograph are the hydraulic tower of Hamilton Square station on the underground electric railway and the chimney stack of the railway power station on the corner of Canning Street. The hydraulic tower, built in 1886 of brick and terracotta in the style of an Italian campanile, housed the water tanks and rams to work the lifts to the underground station. Two of the lifts were electrified in 1936 and one hydraulic lift was kept in reserve till about 1952.

The railway tracks were 103 feet below the street. The panel on the side of the tower read: 'Mersey Railway frequent electric trains to Liverpool & C'. A fascia board beneath the gabled facade read: 'To Liverpool in 3 minutes by frequent electric trains'. The coal-fired power station was built for the Mersey Railway electrification in 1903 and its 270-foot chimney-stack, erected in 56 days, was the tallest structure on the Cheshire side of the Mersey. The power station closed in 1959 when the railway switched to the National Grid, and it took much longer than 56 days to dismantle the chimney in 1961-62. The railway station was surrounded by soot-black, stone-faced, late-Georgian buildings on Hamilton Street and Bridge Street. Beyond the chimney-stack we see the stepped outline of the Mersey Tunnel's Woodside ventilation shaft, and below it the bulk of Shore Road Pumping Station, built in 1886 with three

giant steam beam-engines to draw water out of the railway tunnel. The Andrew Barclay engines had a 1,600-year guarantee against failure, but the pumps were electrified in 1926. Two beam-engines were kept in reserve till 1959 – now one is retained for demonstration. A Birkenhead bus on route 22 from Moreton Shore to Woodside Ferry stops to unload by the glazed canopy outside the station booking hall. Tramway traction poles still serve as lamp posts.

Above right The uniformity of the terraces around **HAMILTON SQUARE** was relieved by projecting bays with Tuscan porticos, as seen here in the centre of the north terrace, and attached Tuscan columns on the projecting 'pavilions' at the ends of the terraces forming the cornerstones of the square. The terraces are built of brick and faced with smooth, square-hewn stone (ashlar), rusticated on the ground floor elevation. The square was originally residential, the home of industrialists, merchants and professional men, including William Laird and his son John, the shipbuilders and founders of Birkenhead, who lived at No 63, the pavilion at the north end of the Hamilton Street frontage. By the 1950s the wealthy had moved out of town and Hamilton Square had become the business centre of Birkenhead. Now the professionals did their business here instead: architects, dentists, doctors, estate agents, insurance agents, merchant bankers and solicitors, together with the offices of the Conservative and Liberal Associations and municipal departments. Nos 10 and 9 Hamilton Square, seen here in 1971, were the offices of Birkenhead Corporation Public Health Department, Children's

Department and Welfare Department. Private residents still lived on upper floors around the square.

Below The black, stone, Georgian-style terraces continued from Hamilton Square into **CLEVELAND STREET** for a short distance, but soon the image faded into two-storey brick terraces of dockland slums. We are looking west along Cleveland Street from the north side of Hamilton Square. The gaunt ruin of Mossop's furniture removals depository in a former Victorian Gothic chapel, destroyed by fire in about 1950, stands on the corner of Argyle Street. This chapel is the backdrop of an engraving of George Train's pioneer tramway on the opening day in 1860 (see overleaf). In this 1954 photograph a Birkenhead bus casually pauses a few yards away from the cast-iron and glass colonnaded shelter spanning the footpath to load a few passengers outward-bound on the counter-clockwise North Circle route 94 via Tollemache Road; these shelters were a characteristic feature of the Birkenhead townscape. The only other vehicle in view is the 'Dan Dare'-style car in the foreground, a 1949 Austin Atlantic A90.

Below The chapel and terraced houses at the corner of Argyle Street and Cleveland Street in the previous picture can be identified as the backdrop of this well-known engraving of **BRITAIN'S FIRST TRAMCAR**, showing the first horse-tram on the opening day of the Birkenhead Street Railway from Woodside Ferry to Birkenhead Park, 30 August 1860. This was the first tramway in Britain. 'Street railways' had been established in several North American cities and this line was promoted by Mr George Train, of Boston, the hatless gentleman on the front steps of the car. The total gestation period for the line was just 25 weeks from the time he applied to Birkenhead Commissioners, or 14 weeks from approval to opening, including shipment of equipment, assembly of the first four cars and laying of tracks. No time or money was wasted: no consultants, no feasibility study, no cost-benefit analysis, no environmental impact assessment, no public inquiry, no Act of Parliament, no Government funding, no contractors, sub-contractors or plant hire! Mr Train shouldered all the cost and risk liability and employed direct labour. It took 59 men with muscles, picks and shovels just six weeks to lay the 2¼ miles of track along the initial route – outward via Shore Road, Argyle Street and Conway Street, and back via Conway Street and Hamilton Street – with kerbside double track in Conway Street and crown-of-the-road single track the rest of the way. The track was laid to the Pennsylvania standard gauge of 5ft 2¼in (later re-gauged to the British standard 4ft 8½in). The service began with four cars – two single-deckers and two open-top double-deckers – which carried twice as many passengers as contemporary horse-buses: 24 seated on each deck and 24 standing strap-hangers in the saloon. The light-green cars were fitted out inside with carpets, cushioned seats, sash windows and slatted sunblinds. *The Illustrated London News* reported: 'The cars move along the line as easily and as smoothly as any first-class railway carriage.' *Contemporary newspaper illustration from the Birkenhead Central Reference Library collection*

Below Only 125 yards and two blocks west of Hamilton Square we are in **CHAPEL STREET** in the slums. These early Victorian terraces were not the kind envisaged by Gillespie Graham in his classical grand plan for Birkenhead; they housed the labourers who built the new town and worked its docks, shipyards, factories and railways.

By 1962 that era of Birkenhead has come to an end but people are still living in this semi-derelict street as the demolition gang moves in on the disused Brunswick Methodist Chapel and lecture hall at the end of the street, fronting Price Street. This chapel is shown on an 1835 map of Birkenhead, standing almost in isolation before the neighbourhood was built up. Heads pop out of doorways and pedestrians stop or turn to watch the photographer record the last days of this humble habitat of the Industrial Age. Perhaps they are wondering why anyone should want a photograph of this unpicturesque subject. Living conditions were grim, but the scene has a certain quaintness like a theatrical set. A leaning gas lamp, still aglow, stands outside the corner shop at the entrance of Brook Street. The houses have stone cornices and string courses, and the three beyond Brook Street have steps with railings up to the front doors in the Georgian tradition. They were the first three houses built in Chapel Street, in about 1840, still in the classical era of the development of Birkenhead, and stood in isolation until building resumed in the industrial 1850s and '60s.

Above right Evening sunlight casts the shadow of a gas lamp across the brick gable wall on the corner of **TAYLOR STREET** (left) and **GEORGE STREET** (right). The breadth of the gable wall (indicating the depth of the rooms), the proportions of the windows, the stone cornices and string courses, the railings, the steps up to the front doors, the basements below the steps and the peeling stucco over the brickwork of the terrace in George Street are a legacy of the late-Georgian or Regency style of construction, which continued into the 1840s and '50s when these terraces were built in the area between Cleveland Street and Canning Street. Once this was a pleasant middle-class residential area when Birkenhead was a new town planned around Hamilton Square, but with the development of dockland the social order changed, family houses became rented tenements and the area fell on hard times. In 1962 people are still living here but in slum conditions due to neglect and deterioration of the fabric. Many of the tenements have been abandoned: the end is near.

Below The main road from Heswall and Woodchurch, the A552, entered Birkenhead on a long descent down the continuous curves of **BOROUGH ROAD** between uniform two-storey terraced houses, broken only by the startling white, Portland stone, classical Central Library of 1934 and a few shops converted from the houses. Jim Miller's barber's shop is on the corner of Vincent Street (left), and two other shops are marked by white canvas canopies further down the terraces. The spire of St John's Church, Huskisson Street, rises above the rooftops on the left, and the tower of Liverpool Cathedral, 2¼ miles away across the river, terminates the view. Side streets rise steeply on each side of Borough Road, which was built in 1850-70 along the winding, wooded Happy Valley that drained into Tranmere Pool just beyond the site of Central station. Two motorcycle combinations (with sidecars) are parked by the left-hand kerb, being prepared for an outing on this fine, peaceful Sunday morning in 1954.

Above Signals mounted on a lamp post in the middle of the road control traffic at the five-way junction of **CHARING CROSS**, viewed here from Whetstone Lane in 1954. Grange Road is to the right, Oxton Road and Grange Road West to the left, and Atherton Street lies ahead over the brow. The latter immediately forks left of the house peering over the brow and Exmouth Street forks right, leading down to dockland, making Charing Cross virtually a six-way junction. Two neo-Classical hotels of the 1840s and two neo-Romantic banks of 1900-02 face each other diagonally across this junction. Bank Buildings dominates the scene with its late-Victorian free-style composition of arches, oriels, turrets and spires forming the apex of the curve from Grange Road West to Atherton Street. It housed Martin's Bank and five shops: a nurseryman, sports outfitter, tobacconist, optician and ladies' costumier. The rounded frontage of the Grange Hotel takes the curve from Grange Road to Atherton Street and displays 'Birkenhead Ales' and 'Grange Hotel' in gilded letters on frames standing proud of the building. The Park Hotel (left foreground) faces the Grange Hotel. The Midland Bank is on the extreme right, and by the bus stop outside it stands a fine example of a surviving

Birkenhead Corporation tramway traction pole with bracket arm, ornamental scrollwork and finial, adapted for street lighting. The Corporation bus at the stop in Atherton Street has come from Port Sunlight via Bebington Road, Derby Road and Whetstone Lane on route 52, and will terminate shortly at Park station.

Below Only a mile from Woodside Ferry, and a quarter of a mile from Charing Cross, the dense mesh of grimy streets suddenly gives way to **BIRKENHEAD PARK**, a green oasis of landscape gardening covering 226 acres and an area of the town half a mile wide and three-quarters of a mile long. The park has been extended from the original 180 acres that opened in 1847, when it was the first municipal public park in the world. The main entrance is a large, noble, Ionic triumphal arch in local sandstone at the corner of Conway Street and Park Road East.

Birkenhead Improvement Commissioners bought this marshy tract, unsuitable for building, as a recreational area for the growing new town, and engaged Sir Joseph Paxton, Britain's leading landscape gardener, to design the layout of the park, while his pupil, Edward Kemp, supervised the groundwork

and landscaping. It took nearly 1,000 men four years to drain the land, dig ponds, create hills from the spoils, plant trees and lay out bowling greens, cricket pitches and tennis courts. There are two large fishponds with islands; the island in the lower pond near the main entrance is accessible by footbridges. This Swiss-style covered footbridge with steps, dating from the opening of the park but much restored and seen here in 1961, is built of timber and stone with a red tiled roof. The town Commissioners paid for the park by selling building plots for the classical, Italianate and Gothic villas that stand within its perimeter, almost lost among the trees, beside the 3-mile winding circuit of Park Drive and the axial Ashville Road. Birkenhead Park rugby ground is at the west end, on Park Road North. On one side of the park rise the leafy streets of Claughton with its fine early-Victorian villas. On the other side of the park a grim grid of terraced houses stretches to dockland.

Right Stretching north-west from the town centre alongside the docks is a criss-cross grid of streets, a mile long and a quarter of a mile wide, laid out by James Gillespie Graham in 1824 and extended north and west by the Improvement Commissioners in 1833. This area was to be developed like Hamilton Square in

the Georgian style of Edinburgh New Town, but only a few isolated terraces dotted the headland by the mid-1840s when funds ran out. Then the grand plan was eclipsed by the needs of the thousands of workers engaged in the development of the town, docks, shipyards, ferries, railways, utility services and the park. The grid layout of streets was built up with mean terraced houses and factories from about 1850, the spaces left for gardens being filled in with back streets and alleyways. **CATHCART STREET** was one of the main cross streets of this layout, traversing the width of the grid at its mid-point, running from Conway Street to the docks. It is seen here from Cleveland Street, with the wooded Prenton Ridge (255 feet) as a backdrop. Ships and cranes towered over the other end of the street behind the camera.

The width of Cathcart Street is a legacy of its classical concept in the grand plan, being one of the main streets of the grid laid out to a width of 60 feet. On the left-hand side were St Peter's Church and Sunday School, Cathcart Street School, the Anchor Inn, a fish and chip shop, a newsagent's shop and a Ministry of Food office, while Birkenhead Co-op had a depot on the right-hand side. Bombed sites form gaps in the street frontage and a burnt ruin stands on the left hand corner of Cleveland Street. The street scene is animated by people, mostly wives and children, enjoying the August sun in 1954. Residents at that time included labourers, stevedores, crane-drivers, shipwrights, a riveter, van-drivers, a radio engineer, a painter and a window-cleaner.

Right Straight and wide for more than a mile, **CLEVELAND STREET** was one of the main thoroughfares running the length of the new town grid laid out in 1824. This was also the 'Line of Docks' of the Birkenhead tramways, which bequeathed a succession of traction poles for use as lamp posts, single electric

lamps being suspended economically over the middle of the road on the long bracket arms that once held the electric wires above the double tram tracks. Line D (for Docks) closed in 1935 and was replaced by the North Circle bus route. The docks lay about 600 yards off to the left of the picture, and we are looking from the Cathcart Street crossing towards Hamilton Square. Beyond the burnt ruin on the right were James Fogg's refreshment rooms, St Nathanial's old age pensioners' rest centre, Irving, Little & Company's paint factory, the North Western public house (named after the London & North Western Railway) and the Mersey Mission to Seamen's Indian Club. Brinley & Company, electrical engineers, manufacturers and wholesalers, had premises on both sides of the street here. In the recess beyond the terraced houses on the left in this 1954 view was Rendel Street (named after the first dock engineer), the entrance to the dock branch of the Mersey road tunnel, a public weighbridge, then Freeman Street. The large building on the corner of Freeman Street and Cleveland Street was the Neptune Works of A. Rutherford & Company Ltd, shipwrights and engineers.

THE DOCKS

We waited by the decayed Regency terrace on Bridge Street, up the slope above Woodside station, and boarded the bus to Wallasey, which lay across the docks. Upstairs the arched ceiling, with timber ribs, was an ochre-stained shade of cream from the haze of pipe and cigarette smoke of the predominantly male clientele of the top deck. The conductor followed us up to collect our fares in his leather shoulder-bag, issuing coloured card tickets from a wooden ticket rack and good-humouredly keeping the passengers entertained. The shipwrights, shop-workers and office clerks were going home at teatime on a December day. Under the black vault of the sky the lamp-lit streets of grey ashlar and red brick took on a picturesque appearance like theatre scenery.

Dockland also took on a new magic by night. As we headed along the straight, drab gauntlet of Cleveland Street we could see, through the gas-lit side streets and over the rooftops, the lit-up superstructure of the great passenger/cargo liners and freighters in Vittoria Dock as they were unloaded, serviced and loaded around the clock for a quick turn-round. The docks began at Woodside and ran inland for 2 miles. A mile from Hamilton Square, Cleveland Street left the built-up area and continued straight on across a desolation of bombed sites, wastelands, junk yards and palisades of sooty railway sleepers or rusty corrugated iron. Here the bus turned right into Duke Street and dipped towards the docks.

A white-coated policeman standing in what looked like a black-and-white-painted oil-drum at the crossing of Corporation Street stopped the road traffic for a long, long goods train to clatter slowly across an ungated level crossing on the BR line to the coal and ore sidings and Beaufort Road wharves. Over the crossing, Duke Street almost lost its way, following an ill-defined path through a maze of railway lines branching out from the main docks line alongside Corporation Road and leading to all the wharves on both sides of the docks. The street lay open to the railway sidings and wasteland of Duke Street Wharf on the left, and was walled off by the large brick sheds on the right, including the ships' chain-testing works. Double railway tracks ran along the middle of the street like tramlines, gleaming in the lamplight, between the two lines of motor traffic, which slowly moved off after the hold-up at the crossing. In the shadowy half-light one of Rea's coal-and-iron-wharf locomotives, a quaint, four-wheel saddle-tank engine, simmered on a curved track in the gateway of a brick shed. The words 'Herron for Ford' appeared overhead in white letters on a blue, enamelled steel advertisement clapped to the weatherboarding of a long, wooden cabin that spanned the street on a steel gantry. This was the machine and control room for Duke Street Bridge, the bascule bridge (rolling lift-bridge or drawbridge) that carried the road and railway across the passage between the East and West Floats. After the bridge house, the huge ballast tank that balanced the bridge loomed overhead out of the darkness and we passed through the box framework of girders that was the bridge itself, with lights reflected on the steel runways, the double railway tracks and the ruffled water in the docks on both sides. The sterns of great ships seemed almost to overhang the cross-docks road on the bridge approaches, illuminated by the wharf lamps, deck and cabin lights, and their superstructures loomed large against the black night sky.

THE WALLASEY PERSPECTIVE

As we rolled off the north end of the bridge and its abutment we were in Wallasey, and the railway tracks fanned out in five directions at the junction of Duke Street and Dock Road. Although we called these the Birkenhead docks, almost half the dock estate was in Wallasey. The docks were built up a creek of the Mersey called Wallasey Pool, with Birkenhead on the south shore and the Wallasey townships of Poulton and Seacombe on the north. The boundary line between the two county boroughs ran along the middle of the Great Float and Wallasey Dock, so you could say we were in

Wallasey halfway across Duke Street Bridge and the other dock crossings.

There were only four roads into Wallasey, and three of them lay across the docks from Birkenhead. Duke Street was the main road crossing of the docks between the two boroughs, halfway along the line of docks. Poulton Bridge, a swing-bridge, spanned the head of the creek between the West Float and Bidston Dock. Tower Road was a causeway along the original dam across the mouth of the creek, with the great pound of the East Float on the inland side with three drawbridges and one swing-bridge spanning the entrances to Egerton Dock, Wallasey Dock and Alfred Dock (two bridges) on the river side. Tower Road was better known as the Four Bridges, the most notorious of the dock crossings because of the likelihood of delay by at least one of the bridges being open for the passage of ships at the busier end of the dock system, especially at Alfred Dock, which was the main river entrance to the system. There was a possible further delay at the main-line railway crossing at Corporation Road, where level crossing gates and a busy junction were controlled by Canning Street North signal cabin. Double railway tracks traversed the length of Tower Road, linking Woodside with Seacombe. This causeway was another of my favourite haunts on Merseyside, for its insular nature, the wide open spaces of granite setts and railway tracks, the dock railway movements and the moving bridges with the passage of ships. There was a seventh bridge, another drawbridge, on Spike Road, a side-road around Egerton Dock spanning the passage between Egerton and Morpeth Docks. Road traffic shared this bridge with long main-line goods trains to and from the GWR Morpeth Dock goods station and marshalling yard. All three dock crossings between Birkenhead and Wallasey and all seven dock bridges carried double railway tracks flush with the paving. All five drawbridges had replaced old swing-bridges in 1931-32.

Wallasey Pool had a history of shipping before the docks were built. Poulton, named after Wallasey Pool, stood at the head of the creek, which was a natural harbour conveniently sited for the neighbouring villages of Wallasey and Liscard when Birkenhead was just a wood and the former island of Wallasey was a peninsula with land access via Leasowe, but cut off by high water. In the 16th and 17th centuries Poulton rivalled the ports of Chester and Liverpool, with a greater tonnage of shipping.

The first docks were built at the mouth of the creek by Woodside in 1844-47 – Morpeth Dock and Egerton Dock – with a locked entrance through Morpeth Lock from the river. These two docks were the smallest, although Morpeth Dock was later enlarged. The Great Float opened in 1860, but it was not till Alfred Dock opened in 1866, with larger locks from the river providing a new entrance to the system, that the Great Float got into full swing. Vittoria Dock was created as an open dock within the East Float in 1909, and Bidston Dock was the last dock to be opened, in 1933, reclaiming the last vestige of the natural creek. The docks were owned and operated by the Mersey Docks & Harbour Board (MDHB) from 1857.

The construction of the docks, with three of the four access roads to Wallasey, rendered the former island less isolated than it had been before, although it could still be cut off by the volume of shipping passing through open dock bridges, closing the cross-docks roads for maybe 20 minutes at a time. Wallaseyans had their first sight of dockland from the top of the bus as it swayed down Oxton Road and Gorsey Lane, Poulton, into the dark gulf: a formidable sight of sky-reaching cranes, tall smoke-stacks and a forest of funnels and masts in black silhouette against the grey, overhanging gloom. Sometimes an up-ended drawbridge would be added to the skyline, and we knew that we could be delayed.

Through force of geography, Wallaseyans saw more of Birkenhead docks than Birkonians did in their daily travels. Six joint Corporation bus routes crossed the docks between the two towns in the 1950s: the 10, 11 and 12 over Duke Street Bridge, the 9 and 18 over Poulton Bridge, and the unlucky 13 over the Four Bridges. While most of Liverpool docks were hidden away behind high walls or railings, Birkenhead docks lay open to the roads, which were inextricably mixed up with the wharves and the dock railways, and the bows and sterns of the big cargo liners loomed large in our everyday comings and goings.

DOCK RAILWAYS

The bus heeled over to right and left as it zig-zagged around the staggered crossing of Dock Road from Gorsey Lane into Duke Street across the maze of railway tracks at this junction. As we traversed Duke Street on the 10, 11 or 12, or Tower Road on the 13, the lower-saloon passengers often looked out at files of railway wagons passing close by the offside windows as goods trains took their place in the normal order of road traffic. The motive power of these trains was the most endearing feature of dockland: short, Emetty, four-wheel, industrial saddle-tank engines, some with wire-basket spark-arresters on their chimneys. They were almost human with their idiosyncrasies and names, among them *Brian*, *Jessie* and *Remus*, *Cyclops* and *Vulcan*, *Tynesider* and *Shamrock*, *Dolgarrog* and *Melsonby No 3*. They chuffed, clanked and waddled along the granite-sett-paved roads with their trains of creaking, groaning wagons alongside the motor traffic, through the tall grass and weeds of Duke Street Wharf, and disturbed the pigeons in the shadows of the giant granaries and mills and their overhead footbridges on Dock Road. Bus route 12 was engulfed in this shadowy, canyon of six-storey granaries and mills, railway sidings, horse-drawn wagons and the strong, sweet smell of grain on its short but eventful journey of contrasts from Seacombe Ferry to Charing Cross, taking in Birkenhead Park on the way.

Birkenhead docks were particularly well served by railways, with access from the LMS & GWR Chester main line and from the Seacombe branch on the London & North Eastern Railway (LNER) line from Wrexham, leading to seven main-line goods stations on the Birkenhead side and two on the Wallasey side; in later BR days these were dedicated to the goods traffic of the Midland, Western and Eastern Regions and were worked by the locomotives of the ancestral companies. Beyond these goods stations and yards, a ramification of 48 miles of MDHB railway tracks extended along the streets and wharves, penetrating almost every nook and cranny with some very tight curves, compounded by wagon turntables with spurs into warehouses.

Large main-line locomotives worked trains along or alongside streets to their dockside goods stations and yards, which were shunted by venerable tank engines that were getting a bit long in the chimney and had been sent into semi-retirement on Birkenhead docks. Morpeth Dock goods station was shunted by the GWR's characteristic 0-6-0 Pannier tank engines. Elsewhere we found veterans of the LNWR, Midland Railway, Lancashire & Yorkshire Railway, North Staffordshire Railway, North London Railway, Great Central Railway, North Eastern Railway and Great Eastern Railway.

An interesting ramification was the access to dockland for goods from the Midland, Great Central and Great Northern, and, after 1923, from the LNER. They penetrated rival LNWR/LMS railway territory as partners in the Cheshire Lines from Manchester to Chester, then over Great Central/LNER metals to Bidston Junction. From their goods sidings at Bidston they ran alongside Beaufort Road and Corporation Road in Birkenhead, giving access to Cavendish Wharf and Duke Street Wharf and leading to the Cheshire Lines' Shore Road goods station at Woodside. Another route from Bidston took them over the Seacombe branch and Slopes branch at Poulton to Bidston Dock and alongside Dock Road to the Cheshire Lines' East & West Float goods station at the corner of Gorsey Lane, Poulton, and to the Great Central's Dock Road goods station at Kelvin Road in Seacombe. The Slopes branch facilitated the development of Bidston Dock in 1933 and its later iron-ore trade.

While the MDHB had its own fleet of four-wheel and six-wheel saddle-tank engines to work its Liverpool dock railways, on the Birkenhead docks the work was done by local private haulage contractors, among them Joseph Perrin & Son Ltd, William J. Lee and Rea Bulk Handling Ltd, with second-hand saddle-tank engines from collieries and mills, rebuilt and hired out or sold by Cudworth & Johnson of Wrexham. Some mills and factories had their own shunting engines. Shunting was also done by horses and hydraulic capstans. The use of draught horses in dockland was the reason why the streets were paved with granite setts and the exclusive railway tracks and sidings with rough boulder-paving.

After the war, diesel road haulage slowly began to eclipse horsepower and railways in dockland, as we can see by the motor lorries in the photographs. Horse and steam traction carried on through the 1950s, but most of the horses and engines had been retired by the end of the decade, although some of the dockside steam engines carried on working till 1964. The dock railways did not live long enough to see steam replaced by diesel, except for Rea's diesel shunters on the iron-ore sidings at Duke Street and Cavendish Wharves and Bidston Dock from 1960, and BR diesels to Morpeth Dock and Beaufort Road.

SHIPPING, TRADE AND INDUSTRY

In dockland ships have right of way over road and rail traffic, which was often held up at high water when ships moved in and out of the docks and the bridges opened for them to pass through. This was one of the routine daily dramas of dockland, and the delay was compensated by the spectacle. A whistle blew, an electric bell trilled and a dim, red light loomed towards us on the end of a long iron gate that swung across the road. Road traffic then began to queue up at each end of the bridge. The low groan of electric machinery commenced as the wooden bridge cabin astride the road began to haul in the massive steel drawbars, which slowly projected through and behind the cabin along rollers on the gantry. The great bridge rolled lethargically back on the bowed end of its base girders, which curved up to the ballast tank, tenons on the bowed segments keying into mortises on a steel runway. The groaning ceased and the bridge slumped to a standstill in an almost vertical position, with the road and railway lines on the bridge deck leading up into the sky. Then we watched the slow procession of one or more ships, with tugs fore and aft, perhaps followed by a coaster, a motor-barge or towed lighters, filing through the passage between the docks. When the convoy was clear, the groaning began again and the bridge lowered at an alarming speed until it was a few yards above the sill of the road, then it paused to change into low gear for a slow descent and boomed gently into position with the railway tracks perfectly lined up. The iron gate swung back and the motor traffic rumbled on its way across the bridge. The whole operation had probably taken about 20 minutes, but it was worth it and was an accepted way of life on the west bank of the Mersey.

The ships we saw in Birkenhead and Wallasey docks were mainly passenger/cargo liners and freighters of the Blue Funnel Line, Clan Line, Ellerman (City) Line, Harrison Line and Lamport & Holt Line, trading mainly with south and east Africa, India, China, Japan and Australia. Chief among them were Alfred Holt's Blue Funnel liners, which were as much a symbol of Birkenhead as the blue Corporation buses. They were big, sturdy ships with upright blue/black funnels and names from Greek mythology. They were always berthed in the East Float and Vittoria Dock, as were the Clan Line steamers, the other principal players in the dockland scene. Birkenhead also harboured ocean-going passenger/cargo liners and freighters of the Anchor Line, Bibby Line, Brocklebank Line, Hain Steamship Company, Hall Line, Henderson Line, Houlder Brothers, India Steamship Company, Irish Shipping Ltd, Larringa Steamship Company, Nippon Yusen Kaisha, North Yorkshire Shipping Company, and Scottish Ore Carriers. All had their appointed berths in the East and West Floats, Vittoria Dock, Morpeth Dock and Bidston Dock. Ocean and coastal tankers served United Molasses, Liverpool Oil Storage Company, Vacuum Oil Works, and Anglo-American Oil Company at the head of the West Float, while short sea and coastal traders berthed in Morpeth Dock, Egerton Dock and Wallasey Dock.

Birkenhead docks were at their busiest in the 1940s, '50s and '60s. Over the 20 years after the war a total of £53 million was spent on enlarging wharfage, cranage and storage at the East Float, Vittoria Dock and Bidston Dock. In 1952 Birkenhead was handling 20 per cent of the trade of the port of Liverpool and, with the decline of the latter's older and smaller southern docks and the continuing development of facilities on the west bank, by 1969 Birkenhead had 40 per cent of tonnage in the port. Birkenhead's catchment area was generally the Midlands and Wales by virtue of its railway connections, while Liverpool mainly served the North of England.

Birkenhead exported Midland manufactures, machinery, iron and steel, motor vehicles, pottery and chemicals, and its better road and rail access gave it an advantage over Liverpool's walled-in docks, behind the superstructure of the Overhead Railway, for the handling of bulk cargoes such as coal and iron-ore and bulky cargoes such as cranes and railway locomotives and carriages. Coal came from Welsh, Midland and Yorkshire mines and was shipped from Vittoria Creek, Duke Street Wharf and Cavendish Wharf to Ireland, while steam coal went straight into ships' bunkers in dock or was shipped as cargo to overseas bunkering stations. This was still the Steam Age on land and sea. To see a main-line steam railway locomotive hoisted on board ship was another of the routine dramas of dockland. Birkenhead exported locomotives from Beyer, Peacock, of Manchester, and the Vulcan Foundry, Newton-le-Willows, to Africa, India, the Far East and South America. They came by road through the Mersey Tunnel and were stored on mixed-gauge tracks on Cavendish Wharf, before being hoisted on board by a giant floating crane and shipped as deck cargo. Railway carriages were also stored on Cavendish Wharf sidings and shipped on deck, boarded up against sea damage like the locomotives.

The main imports to Birkenhead were grain from the Americas, Australia, India and Europe, livestock and frozen meat, mainly from Ireland, heavy oil, molasses, timber and iron-ore. The huge granaries built in 1868 on the East Float at Seacombe brought the inland millers to the port around the turn of the century to build their towering, steam roller-mills on the dockside, producing flour and animal foods: Buchanan's, Paul Brothers, Joseph Rank, Uveco and Vernon's. The combined mills of Birkenhead and Liverpool made Merseyside the biggest flour-milling centre in Europe and the second largest in the world after Minneapolis in the North American prairies. Much North American grain came as ballast cargo in passenger liners to Liverpool docks and was transhipped by barge to Birkenhead docks. Seacombe mills formed a long quadrangle around a barge dock. Grain was unloaded from ships and barges by bucket elevators and pneumatic elevators. Molasses were mixed with low-grade grain and the wastes from refining flour to produce cattle food. The flour and cattle food left the mills in 2½cwt sacks by coaster, railway and lorry – 70,000 sacks a week in 1948.

Birkenhead had the main quarantine lairage for foreign cattle imported to Britain. Cattle, sheep, goats and pigs were landed here in their thousands on the north end of Woodside Landing Stage and at Wallasey Landing Stage on the river wall between Woodside and Seacombe. They were kept in sheds at Morpeth Dock and Wallasey Dock to recover from their voyage and for quarantine and inspection. There was a cattle market, slaughterhouse and meat store at Woodside, and the animals left the lairage by train, either on the hoof for rearing on British farms or as frozen meat to Smithfield and other meat markets. As late as 1955 cattle and meat trains left Shore Road lairage sidings with 150 to 200 vans a day, and they had priority over all other goods trains from Birkenhead. By-products of the slaughterhouses provided the raw materials for the tannery and glue factory at Lower Tranmere.

Heavy oil and molasses were stored in the jungle of circular tanks around the head of the West Float. The oils were blended to different grades and grease extracted for lubrication of marine, industrial and automotive engines, and refined for bunker fuel in the growing number of motorships. Iron-ore unloaded at Cavendish Wharf and, from 1951, at Bidston Dock went to the nearby Bidston Steel Works (1947-87) and by train to John Summers's Steel Works at Shotton, Flintshire, and steel works in the Black Country. The most important allied shipping industry in dockland was the Manganese Bronze & Brass

Company on Dock Road, Poulton, which used imported ores to cast ships' screws. The firm had expanded here from London's dockland in 1942. We could see the giant propellers, up to 25 feet across, stored in the yard. This firm equipped all the big liners and most of the British merchant fleet of the 20th century, including the RMS *Queen Mary* and RMS *Queen Elizabeth*, and the entire Royal Navy in the Second World War. It was renamed Stone Manganese Marine in 1963 and is still there today, making even larger screws for larger ships.

The dust and dirt and din of dockland, of loading coal, unloading cattle and ores, milling grain, smoking funnels and chimneys in a land of granite paving, grim brick walls and steel bridges, cranes and ships, was nonetheless grist to the mill of the spectator, as it was to the thousands of men employed there. The odious odours and the noises were offset by the strong, sweet smells from the mills on Dock Road, the pervading salty tang in the fresh wind off the water, the cries of the seabirds circling overhead, and the background symphony of steam whistles and air horns from shipping moving through the docks and up, down and across the big river outside the lock gates.

Gateway to dockland: the rugged, grimy, stone gatehouse with the date stone 1868 stood guard at the southern entrance to dockland in **SHORE ROAD, BIRKENHEAD**, at the foot of Hamilton Street (left). The notice boards tell us that this was a private road of the Mersey Docks & Harbour Board giving access to Morpeth, Egerton, Wallasey and Alfred Docks. Police stood sentry here checking vehicles entering the dock estate. Most of the dock trade had gone when this picture was taken in 1976, cranes stood idle, wharves and warehouses were empty and parked cars blocked the weedy railway tracks, but all the fabric of the old Shore Road of the 1950s and before was still there. We see the transit sheds alongside Morpeth Branch Dock on the right, the Cheshire Lines goods station on the left, and the caged-up gas lamps, still aglow. Shore Road had the last gas street lights in Wirral; they were finally snuffed out in 1986.

The three-track railway along the right-hand side of Shore Road ran sidings to four premises within the purview of this scene. A single-line siding entered this end of the goods station. Pacific Road was gated and double-track sidings ran through the black iron gates at this end of the transit sheds into Pacific Road to run around Morpeth Branch Dock. A single-track coal siding led into the Mersey Railway power and pumping station behind the wall on the left. The three tracks along Shore Road ended in three sidings into the Woodside cattle lairage to the right of the gatehouse. As late as 1955 cattle and meat trains left the lairage sidings, with 150 to 200 vans a day. A stone arch in the wall at this end of the Cheshire Lines warehouse was the dockers' entrance, complete with booking office, to a 170-yard-long underground passage sloping down to the mezzanine level of Hamilton Square station on the Mersey Railway. This entrance closed with the demise of the docks but is still there today, white-tiled and lit as an emergency exit from the station.

Right This remarkable bird's-eye view of **BIRKENHEAD DOCKS** from above Woodside in about 1958 shows the whole of dockland between Birkenhead (left) and Wallasey (right), running north-west up the old creek, Wallasey Pool. (The previous photograph was taken in the bottom left foreground.) In the foreground are the Mersey Cattle Wharf, Woodside lairage and the Mersey Tunnel ventilation shaft on the river wall. Shore Road follows the old shoreline of the creek with the triple railway tracks serving the lairage, the Mersey Railway power station (with its tall smoke-stack), warehouses and dockside transit sheds. Behind the sheds lie Morpeth Branch Dock and Morpeth Dock with their entrance lock from the river, leading on to Egerton Dock beyond the drawbridge. These are the oldest docks in the system, dating from 1847, although Morpeth Dock had since been enlarged.

Next to these docks to the right is an island with the GWR's Morpeth Dock goods station (nearer the river) and the LMS sidings. The next two docks to the right are Wallasey Dock and the smaller Alfred Dock, a vestibule dock with the main entrance locks to the system. Behind these docks, across the view, runs Tower Road on a causeway with four bridges linking Birkenhead with Wallasey. Beyond Tower Road lies the expanse of the Great Float with its branch, Vittoria Dock, on the left. Just beyond Vittoria Dock is Duke Street Bridge carrying the main road across the docks and dividing the Great Float into the East and West Floats. Wallasey mills are on the right of the East Float and Birkenhead mills on the left of the West Float. At the head of the West Float is Poulton Bridge, spanning the passage to Bidston Dock, the last of the docks to be opened, in 1933. Beyond lies Bidston Moss, and we can see the white of the sandhills at Leasowe on the Wirral coast of the Irish Sea, which forms the horizon of the view. *Williamson Art Gallery & Museum, Birkenhead*

Below left In **MORPETH DOCK** the autumn afternoon sunshine catches two hibernating passenger ferries of the Isle of Man Steam Packet Company, *Tynwald* (left) of 1947 and *Snaefell* of 1948, and silhouettes a Cock tug of the Liverpool Screw Towage & Lighterage Company. Also in dock are three John Monks coasters and a small Fred Everard coaster. All seven vessels in this 1962 scene are steamers. The Isle of Man ships were always handsome vessels, like small-scale Cunard liners. Morpeth Dock and Egerton Dock were the oldest docks in Birkenhead: Sir Philip Egerton, MP for Cheshire, laid the foundation stone of the dock entrance in 1844 and Lord Morpeth, Chief Commissioner of Woods and Forests (who held the legal right to reclaimed land for the Crown), opened the two docks in 1847.

Morpeth Dock was the original entrance to the Great Float, with an entrance lock from Woodside Basin on the river, till Alfred Dock opened in 1866. It was originally quite narrow for an entrance dock, and all the area we see in this picture was created when the dock was successively enlarged four times between 1853 and 1872 to 16 acres, with 1½ miles of quays. Woodside Basin was converted to Morpeth Branch Dock in 1870. Steamers on the trade routes to South Africa, India and China used this dock exclusively till Vittoria Dock opened in 1909. Some transit sheds were converted to cattle and sheep sheds as part of Woodside lairage.

In the 1950s some Ellerman, Henderson and Bibby Line ships were still berthing in Morpeth Dock, otherwise it was used for short sea and coastal traffic and berthing idle ships, tugs and dredgers and the Douglas and New Brighton ferries laid up during the winter off-season. Wallasey Corporation Ferries had a Marine Department on Morpeth Dock for repairs and maintenance, and the Ministry of Transport also had a Mercantile Marine Office here. From Morpeth Dock pier head the One O'clock Gun, a Hotchkiss naval anti-aircraft six-pounder, aimed at Liverpool, was fired by electric relay from Bidston Observatory as a time check for ships to set their chronometers; it echoed over Merseyside at 1pm daily, rousing gulls and pigeons to flight. The gun, by which Merseysiders set their watches, was last fired in 1969.

Right From the opening of the railway to the docks in 1847 railwaymen called it **THE SOUGH** (pronounced 'suff'), meaning a trench, an approach or a horizontal entrance to a mine. The four-track goods line cut diagonally under the town grid of streets from Blackpool Street Junction on the Chester main line to Brook Street Junction, where tracks diverged around the docks. The Sough tunnelled under Haymarket and ran in a cutting below street level to Bridge Street. This 1954 view from Cleveland Street bridge to Bridge Street bridge shows the dockland end of The Sough, where the tracks spread out. Our viewpoint is the top of the wooden stairs through the door in the wall of Cleveland Street bridge, leading down to the brick huts between the tracks.

In the smoke-diffused sunshine of a Birkenhead morning, the guard of a dock-bound goods train leans over the back of his brake-van. On the right are sidings running into the GWR Town goods station at the west end of Canning Street; its clerestory roof can just be seen peering over Bridge Street bridge. From this point the railway tracks fanned out: right to Shore Road, Egerton Dock, E Bridge and Morpeth Dock, straight on to Tower Road and Seacombe, and left to Vittoria Dock, Duke Street, Cavendish Wharf and Beaufort Road. There were 48 miles of railway track along dock roads and wharves, with sidings encircling every dock. The docks were served by the LMS, GWR, Cheshire Lines and LNER, all with their own goods stations and marshalling yards. Beyond those points local movements and dockside shunting were left to privately owned industrial saddle-tank locomotives. In the background we see the Central Hydraulic Tower (centre) on Tower Road, and the funnels of big ships in Alfred Dock (right).

Below Grime, rust, smoke, steam and decrepitude flavour this 1962 industrial railway idyll in **THE SOUGH** between Canning Street and Bridge Street. A steam locomotive simmers in the shade of Bridge Street bridge in the spring sunshine during its midday siesta between duties in dockland, its outline suggestive of an LMS Class 3F 0-6-0 tank engine. Smoke rises from the stove chimney of an ex-Midland Railway clerestory-roofed carriage, on a siding with a van, used as a mess hut and store for the track gang. Beside it a short carriage, perhaps an ex-six-wheeler, sits on sleepers between the tracks, in use as a store. The picture was taken from the well-worn granite-paved crossing of Canning Street beside the GWR Town goods station (left). The two tracks in the foreground are the main-line link with the Cheshire Lines' Shore Road goods depot, Shore Road sidings to the lairage and the street tracks over E Bridge to the LNWR/LMS South Reserve and Manchester sidings. The two tracks on the right lead to Egerton Dock, with wagon turntables into the LNWR/LMS warehouse there.

On the far side of Bridge Street Bridge stand the Neptune Works of A. Rutherford & Co Ltd, described on the gable wall as 'Ship Repairers, Sheet Metal Workers, Coppersmiths, Plumbers & Ship Painters'. They were also marine engineers, boiler-makers, electrical engineers, sawmillers, dunnage suppliers, yacht, barge, launch and boat builders, ship and yacht outfitters and ironmongers. They also made ships' lifeboats, masts and engine parts.

Bottom This marshalling yard and warehouse at **MORPETH DOCK GOODS STATION**, developed in 1861-69 on a man-made island between the docks and the River Mersey, was the farthest north outpost of the GWR empire. The view is significant in showing Liverpool's impressive waterfront buildings in the background, just over three-quarters of a mile away across the river. The GWR aspired to reach Liverpool but never quite made it, its drive to the Mersey metropolis expiring in this windswept yard within sight of the waterfront. The GWR map showed a solid red line from Birkenhead to Liverpool, but that was the Mersey Railway connection for passengers. For just three months of 1909 GWR buses carried passengers between Woodside station and Liverpool hotels by ferry.

Goods were shipped across the river by barge from a basin inside Morpeth Dock warehouse to the GWR warehouses at Duke's Dock and Manchester Dock, Liverpool, until 1922. Goods were also barged direct to and from ships berthed in other docks or anchored in the river. The warehouse (right) was rebuilt in 1929, when the barge basin was filled in and the marshalling yard was enlarged to a capacity of 850 wagons. The GWR had an office in James Street, Liverpool, and a total of four railless goods depots in the city, from which lorries and vans brought goods to the railhead at Morpeth Dock. Wallasey Landing Stage on the river wall off Morpeth Dock goods yard (actually in Birkenhead but next to Wallasey Dock) was built for the company in 1876 for shipping GWR goods. The stage was also envisaged as a GWR passenger ferry landing place till that idea was eclipsed by the extension of the main line to Woodside Ferry.

In the long rays of summer evening sunshine in 1962, ex-GWR 4-6-0 No 6959 *Peatling Hall*, from Old Oak Common shed in west London, raises steam for its return trip to London with the 8.20pm fast freight, named 'The General', to Paddington, initially traversing street tracks across E Bridge and Canning Street, with much binding and squealing of flanges. The Great Western had 11 named fast freights to or from Birkenhead docks, among them 'The Meat' to Smithfield. The GWR had its own Smithfield goods depot beneath the Central Markets in London with access through the underground Metropolitan Railway to sidings between Farringdon and Aldersgate.

Right The Zillah Shipping Company's motor coaster *Freshfield* (518 gross tons) of 1954, at the north quay of **EGERTON DOCK** with collision damage to its starboard bridge, and a John Monks steam coaster at the west quay are mirrored in the calm water in spring midday sunshine in 1962. In the background is the profile of D Bridge on Tower Road, with its ballast tank at one end to help lift the drawbridge spanning the passage to the East Float. Egerton Dock was named after Sir Philip Egerton, MP for Cheshire, who laid the foundation stone for the docks scheme, and was built by James Rendel in 1844-47, being one of the first two Birkenhead docks to be opened, together with Morpeth Dock. Unlike Morpeth Dock, it remained unchanged to become the smallest dock in the Birkenhead system at just over 4 acres with 700 yards of quays. In the foreground can be seen the original stonework and cast iron dock furniture. In latter years the dock was used only for coastal trades and ships laid up idle or awaiting sale; many left Morpeth Dock and Egerton Dock for the shipbreakers.

Below Viewed from the footbridge over the busy railway crossing at the east end of Corporation Road, with its long, slow freight trains, **TOWER ROAD** was a half-mile-long causeway, with bridges, across the widest part of the docks at the mouth of Wallasey Pool. The route included four bridges, and local people called this road the 'Four Bridges' rather than Tower Road. The first bridge from Birkenhead was the drawbridge, or rolling-lift bridge, in this 1954 view, spanning the passage between Egerton Dock (right) and the East Float (left). There was also a drawbridge at Wallasey Dock and a swing-bridge and a drawbridge at Alfred Dock. As at least one of these bridges was usually open for shipping, most road traffic between Birkenhead and Wallasey used Duke Street Bridge or Poulton Bridge.

A gas lamp hangs from a wall bracket on our left, but electric lighting on 1950s concrete lamp posts has taken over the illumination of the road. In the right foreground, two horses in tandem, known as a 'Liverpool team', are pulling a heavy load of four railway axles; a pre-war Fordson lorry is parked behind it. Double railway tracks from The Sough ran the length of Tower Road with sidings to all docks. In the foreground a single-track siding swings left into a dockyard on the East Float, and double tracks lead off right to Shore Road, Morpeth Branch Dock and Woodside lairage. Over the bridge double-track sidings to the right run along the north side of Egerton Dock, where we can see lines of trucks and vans. A little further on to the right are the tracks leading to the LNWR/LMS South Reserve and Manchester sidings on the far side of the transit sheds.

Above   Silhouetted against the gleam on the water of **EGERTON DOCK** and the smoky, industrial townscape in the backlight of a grey morning in 1954, the lone figure of a dock labourer in cloth cap and hobnail boots walks off D Bridge on Tower Road on his way to work in the docks. He is walking beneath the superstructure of the drawbridge spanning the passage between Egerton Dock and the East Float. The girders of the gantry for the elevated control cabin and its stairway access are to the left of the picture, and a segment of the arc of the rolling section of the bridge is in the top right-hand corner. The backlight picks out the dock railway tracks along the road and the line of studs, or tenons, that secured the mortised arc of the bridge as it rolled; a huge, overhead ballast tank at the top of the arc almost balanced the weight of the bridge.

The steam barge *D. W. Williams* is in dock at the north quay. At the far end of the dock we can just see the outline of E Bridge and its elevated cabin spanning the passage from Morpeth Dock. The landmarks in the background are (from left to right) the smoke-stacks of the Mersey Railway power station and John Marsden & Sons' brass foundry, the hydraulic tower on Hamilton Square station, the Sidney Street ventilation shafts on the Mersey road tunnel, and the clock tower of Birkenhead Town Hall.

Below   The boundary line between the county boroughs of Birkenhead (right) and Wallasey (left) ran along the middle of **WALLASEY DOCK** and the Great Float. Wallasey Dock was originally a low-water basin on the river, built in 1863 to give access to coasters at all states of the tide, but the periodic sluicing with water from the Great Float failed to stop the basin silting up with river mud. The low-water basin was therefore walled up, dredged and converted to Wallasey Dock in 1877-78. About 1880 the import of foreign animals at the Mersey Cattle Wharf at Woodside lairage outgrew the accommodation there, and Wallasey Landing Stage for GWR goods then also came to be used for landing livestock. The warehouses at the far left end of Wallasey Dock became the Wallasey lairage, while the Woodside lairage was extended to converted transit sheds at Morpeth Dock to house cattle and sheep to supply the cattle market, slaughterhouse and meat store at Woodside.

The calm waters of Wallasey Dock mirror the chimney of the pumping station, built in 1890 on the Mersey wall to impound water from the river at a higher level in the Birkenhead dock system, thus providing deeper water for bigger ships and replacing water lost through locking down into the river through Morpeth Dock and Alfred Dock. This system was a success, but it was no advantage to Wallasey Dock itself, as most of the river-borne mud settled in its still waters, which therefore never saw the bigger ships that used the Great Float. Its 13 acres of water and 1,500 yards of quays, used by smaller ships carrying grain and general cargo on short sea and coastal routes, was generally a scene of peaceful inactivity. Cereal merchants and the Cement Marketing

Company had stores here, as well as the offices of HM Customs & Excise and the Mersey Docks & Harbour Board's traffic manager. The steam pumping station next to the chimney shut down in 1955 to be replaced by the new electric pumping station seen here being built alongside in 1954.

Right In 1954 a queue of road traffic for D Bridge on Tower Road stretches back to **C BRIDGE** at the entrance to Wallasey Dock. In the line of vehicles we see one of Henry Cox's coaches, of New Brighton – a 1939 Harrington-bodied Leyland Tiger PS2 in cream and maroon livery. The car at the front is a 1951 Austin A70 Hereford. The wooden bridge cabin spans the road on a gantry, and contains the machine room and control room for the drawbridge. Behind it is the huge ballast tank on the rolling section of the drawbridge to counter-balance its weight when it was opened for shipping. A wisp of smoke trails from the chimney stack and hydraulic tower elegantly disguised as an Italianate clock tower, a landmark of dockland. This is the Central Hydraulic Power Station, opened in 1863, which, through a system of water pipes, powered hydraulic machinery to work swing-bridges, lock gates, cranes, capstans and warehouse lifts and hoists. Drawbridges, installed in 1931-32, were worked by electric power. The tower is soot-black, rock-faced, machicolated and castellated with a lantern spire. It was taller before the war, with a second lantern, which toppled in the 1940 Christmas air raid. The tower was designed by John Hartley, the Mersey Docks engineer (1860-61) in the style of his famous father Jesse Hartley's picturesque industrial architecture in Liverpool dockland.

Below C Bridge is seen here from the other end, as motor traffic from Wallasey to Birkenhead rumbles over the broad acres of granite setts, jolts over the maze of railway tracks and stops to wait while the bridge opens for the passage of a tug with a ship. A dockside railway locomotive steams in from the left to join the queue of vehicles waiting for the bridge to come down. C Bridge spanned the waterway between Wallasey Dock (left) and the East Float (right), on the Four Bridges route across the docks. When the ship has passed, the groaning machinery will lower the bridge to a few yards above the sill of the road, then change gear for a slow descent and a gentle boom into position, with the railway tracks perfectly lined up. A long iron gate will swing open and the traffic, including the locomotive, will be able to move across the bridge into Birkenhead. At the back of the traffic queue we can see (from left to right) a 1938 Austin Goodwood car, a 1938 Fordson van and a 1954 Ford Popular car. From 1955 buses on the new joint Wallasey/Birkenhead Corporation peak-time service 13 from Trafalgar Road, Egremont, to Central station, Birkenhead, were sometimes among the lines of vehicles queuing at the four bridges along Tower Road. The masts and a derrick of a ship loading at Tower Quay at the east end of the East Float can be seen over the roof of the transit shed and the gaunt, bomb-damaged Gothic brick and stone engine-house of the Central Hydraulic Power Station on the right.

Above It's high water in the Mersey, the bridge is up and the Rea steam tug *Dongarth* of 1922 leads a procession of cargo ships through **ALFRED DOCK**, its towlines secured to the bow of Alfred Holt's Blue Funnel liner *Polydorus* (455 feet, 7,671 gross tons) of 1944, bound for Vittoria Dock. Berthed on the left is the Shaw Savill & Albion passenger liner *Gothic*, pictured just four months after it carried Queen Elizabeth and Prince Philip on a five-month cruise from Jamaica to Australasia and Aden on their 1953-54 tour of the Commonwealth following the 1953 Coronation. (The Royal Yacht *Britannia* was not commissioned till 1954, when it took the Royal couple on the last leg of the tour to Malta, Gibraltar and London.) Two other ships can be seen to port and astern of *Polydorus* waiting in Alfred Dock to file through this gap past A Bridge, the fourth bridge on Tower Road, into the East Float. *Dongarth* is moving

slowly through the passage opened by the raised bridge, and the pedestrians on Tower Road are compensated by this spectacle that is the cause of their delay, though some have come just to watch the ships. The shortest bridge delay would be 10 minutes, but a bridge might be up for 40 minutes for a procession of big ships like this to pass through.

Alfred Dock and its entrance locks from the river were built in 1858-66 as an 8½-acre vestibule dock and a larger, northern entrance to the Great Float in succession to the congested narrow southern entrance through Morpeth and Egerton Docks. Traffic in Birkenhead docks had been torpid, but from the opening of this dock in 1866 trade boomed. New entrance locks to Alfred Dock and a second passage from this dock into the East Float were opened in 1928. As a vestibule to the Birkenhead system, Alfred Dock was a base for three tug companies: the Alexandra Towing Company, Liverpool Screw Towing & Lighterage Company, and Rea Towing Company. A small amount of loading and servicing was also carried on at its 611 yards of quays.

Left On the sullen, black, oily water in the north-west corner of Alfred Dock in 1962 we find these sturdy, wooden, motor launches called 'gig boats', whose crews handled the ropes of ships entering and leaving the docks. The third and fourth bridges on the Four Bridges route across the docks were B Bridge, a swing-bridge, and A Bridge, a drawbridge, spanning the two passages between Alfred Dock and the East Float. Beyond the drawbridge (left) and the dock gateman's hut (right) lie the waters of the East Float, and in the background are the transit sheds and warehouses on the Birkenhead side.

Right Wallasey looks at Birkenhead across the waters of the East Float on a glorious summer's evening in 1962 with the Central Hydraulic Tower (left), the James Fisher motor coaster *Bay Fisher* of 1958 at **TOWER WHARF**, an Alexandra tug and a Cock tug astern, and, in the background, a Rea tug berthed alongside the East Float goods station at the end of Cathcart Street. The broad canyon of Cathcart Street (right) leads the eye to the backdrop of Prenton Ridge.

Below **EAST FLOAT GOODS STATION**, built in 1857, at first doubled as a passenger station for emigrants to Australia, who were housed in the cellars while awaiting embarkation. The station was built by the Birkenhead, Lancashire & Cheshire Junction Railway and passed in succession to the London & North Western Railway, then the London Midland & Scottish Railway. The warehouse had two floors above ground and a loading basin for barges, entered by a brick arch under the larger second gable. The barge dock was filled in when the transhipment of railway goods by barge ended in 1922. In 1954 the ICI steam barge *Barnton*, built in 1944 for the Weaver Navigation, is berthed at the colonnaded east wharf. Road access was by Cathcart Street on the west side. On the extreme right of the picture is the familiar outline of a Blue Funnel cargo liner in the Far Eastern trade, its upright, black-topped blue funnel as familiar a trademark of Birkenhead as the blue Corporation buses. The scene is viewed from Tower Wharf, with a 3-ton hand crane and original iron bollards and chains.

Above Three steam tugs of J. H. Lamey Ltd surround the **EAST FLOAT** goods station, and beyond the swing-bridge the floating crane *Mammoth* loads a Clan liner in Vittoria Dock, which was an open basin within the East Float. *Mammoth*, owned by the Mersey Docks & Harbour Board, was Dutch-built in 1920 with twin smoke-stacks and a 200-foot jib that could lift up to 200 tons. This 1962 photograph was taken from D Bridge on Tower Road.

Below **VITTORIA DOCK** was built in 1905-09 and was home to Alfred Holt's Blue Funnel Line (with its own works

department), Brocklebank Line, Clan Line Steamers, and their subsidiaries Houston Line and Scottish Shire Line, all mainly engaged in the Far Eastern trade. The big ships are masking the transit sheds, and the cranes and derricks are in full swing unloading cargoes from Blue Funnel and other freighters on to Vittoria Wharf and over the side into barges. Two ICI steam barges and a motor barge lie alongside the ship on the left, and two Lamey steam tugs are manoeuvring the floating crane *Fender* on the right. This busy 1953 scene was typical of Birkenhead docks in the post-war period, when, with investment in wharfage, cranage and storage, they increased their share of tonnage in the port of Liverpool to 20 per cent by 1952 and 40 per cent by 1969. As part of this programme Vittoria Dock was extended west towards Duke Street in 1960, covering the disused Vittoria Creek coal basin. *Valentine's postcard*

Below Morning sunlight penetrates the gloom over Wallasey Pool, a creek of the Mersey now transformed by the dust and din of dockland to the Great Float, divided by Duke Street Bridge into the East and West Floats. As we look east down the East Float from Duke Street Bridge in 1954, the sunlight silhouettes an Ellerman Line cargo ship loading at Vittoria Wharf, Birkenhead (right), and lights up the flour mills and granaries on the Wallasey side of the creek at Seacombe (left). In the background beyond the warehouses is the jungle of masts, derricks and cranes at Alfred Dock and Wallasey Dock.

The Great Float opened in 1860, and the East Float section was 60 acres in extent with 2½ miles of quays. Ships of the Blue Funnel Line, Ellerman Line, Clan Line, Lamport & Holt Line, Anchor Line, Brocklebank Line and Houston Line berthed in the East Float with cargoes to and from Africa, India, Burma and China.

Above Grain arrived by ship from North and South America, Australia, India and Europe and was stored and processed in Seacombe's giant granaries and mills on the **EAST FLOAT**, in a 1962 scene reminiscent of a port on the Great Lakes. The oldest warehouses here were built in 1868 to store grain before it was taken by train to inland mills. As the grain trade grew, dockside warehouses and transit sheds bulged with grain, so the inland millers moved to the dockside to process the grain straight from the ship, as flour and cattle food was lighter and less bulky to store and transport. Buchanan's built the first mills here in 1893, and others were built around the Great Float over the next 21 years, among them Vernon's, Rank's and Spiller's Uveco Mills. Paul Brothers' Homepride Flour Mills are marked by the chimney on the left. Beyond are the grain warehouses of 1868 and a colossal new concrete grain silo belonging to the Liverpool Grain Store & Transit Company. Merseyside was the biggest flour-milling centre in Europe and second in the world after Minneapolis in the North American prairies. In the autumn afternoon sunshine we see (from the left) the Belgian ship *Schelde* berthed at Buchanan's Mills, two smoking J. H. Lamey tugs lying alongside the Irish ship *Irish Rowan* at Homepride Mills, a third Lamey tug at the old granary wharf, and a third grain freighter at the new silo. In the distance Alfred Dock Bridge is up as a large ship passes through. A fifth ship loads at Vittoria Wharf, Birkenhead, on the right.

Right The quaint old dockside railway locomotive *Cyclops*, an 0-4-0 with outsize buffers and a narrow saddle-tank, shunted the Mersey Cattle Wharf, Seacombe mills and other industrial premises in dockland. In 1954 she is being watered in William J. Lee's single-road, two-engine **SEACOMBE SHED** off Birkenhead Road (left), on the north side of Alfred Dock. The shed was built in 1918 on a siding off the double-track coal line along the east side of Birkenhead Road to Seacombe Ferry, taking coal for the ferry steamers and serving coal yards between the terraced houses on the west side of the road. In the opposite direction tracks from this shed led directly along Tower Road over the Four Bridges or along Dock Road in the shadow of the granaries and mills.

Cyclops was one of the oldest locomotives on the docks in the 1950s, having been built in 1895 by Hudswell Clark at Leeds. It was one of several second-hand industrial locomotives rebuilt and owned by Cudworth & Johnson of Wrexham and leased to the Birkenhead dockside haulage contractors Joseph Perrin & Son Ltd, based at a shed on Shore Road. W. J. Lee had been contractors with horses from 1854 and with steam from 1885. In the 1950s they operated the second-hand Hunslet 0-4-0 saddle-tank locomotive *Shamrock* of 1886, the oldest engine on the docks until its retirement in 1960. For its size, *Cyclops* could haul long trains along the streets, and soldiered on, with its melodious chime whistle echoing around the canyon of mills and warehouses, till 1964. The pit-prop across the buffer-beam is for shunting wagons on an adjacent track!

Above The granaries and mills tower in the background of this general 1954 view of **DOCK ROAD, SEACOMBE**, seen from the junction with the tracks leading off left to Tower Road near Alfred Dock Bridge. Not only was this the dock road along the Wallasey side of the creek, but Dock Road was also its proper name. Bibby Brothers, the Liverpool shipping line, had engineers' stores in the twin, single-storey, clerestory-roofed, stone-built sheds on the left, fenced off by sooty railway sleepers. From this junction three tracks ran along the south side of the road past the mills. The large shed behind the lorries on the right is the Great Central Railway/LNER Dock Road goods station, and a line from the goods yard joined the Dock Road tracks between the Bibby Line stores and the Swan Hotel (centre). The goods depot was also approached from the opposite direction by double tracks off Birkenhead Road opposite Lee's loco shed, crossing Kelvin Road into the yard.

Below The stark bulk of the bomb-damaged east end of the blackened-brick 1868 wharfside granaries towers over Dock Road in 1954. Pigeons feeding on the granite setts and windowsills were roused to flight by the occasional passing train on the weed-grown rails in the boulder-paving in the shadow of the granaries. These original six-storey granaries on the East Float were the first in the world to use hydraulic elevators and hoists. In the late 1890s the greater part of the granaries was converted to mills as Wallasey and Birkenhead began to process most of the imported grain. Those on the left belong to the Liverpool Grain Storage & Transit Company, while the chimney marks the Homepride flour mills, joined on to the west end of the old granaries. In the background we see Buchanan's flour and cattle food mills, which line both sides of Dock Road. These dockside warehouses were badly damaged by bomb blast and fire in the 1940 Christmas blitz. On the railway tracks at this end of the granaries stands an old LNWR single-ended brake-van; there were very few pre-Grouping (pre-1923) brake-vans left by this time. A Leyland Octopus four-axle flat-bed lorry gleams in the sunlight,

parked beside the wasteland that stretches to the right – the undeveloped, unofficial buffer zone that partly insulated dockside industry from residential Seacombe.

Right From beside a railway brake-van in the shadow of the granaries, we are now looking across the sett-paved, gas-lit **DOCK ROAD, SEACOMBE**, to a huddle of industry amid the wasteland between the dockside and the residential streets of Seacombe: a manure works, a steel foundry and engineering works on the west side of Kelvin Road. The nearest buildings are the manure works of Currie, Rowlands & Co, who occupied the site and buildings of the old Seacombe Pottery in 1894 and enlarged the works to

4 acres, producing compound fertilisers. Beyond we can see part of the sheet metal works of H. A. Harben & Co, served by sidings from the Great Central Railway/LNER goods station, just off the picture to the right behind the brake-van. Currie, Rowlands had its own railway locomotive, the 1947 Hudswell Clark 0-4-0 saddle-tank *Kelvinside*, laid up in 1961 and scrapped in 1964. The first commercial ship to enter Birkenhead docks when they opened in 1847 was the barque *Oregon* of Glasgow, bringing a cargo of guano from Patagonia for the Peruvian Phospo Guano Works in Havelock Street, off Wheatland Lane, Seacombe, the forerunner of Currie, Rowlands' manure works.

Below Amid the hum of milling machinery, the high-level footbridges link the giant mills and granaries of **HOMEPRIDE FLOUR MILLS**. Also seen in this 1954 view is the grain elevator rising from Grain Warehouse Dock, enclosed within the quadrangle of buildings, while railway vans wait to load sacks of flour on the tracks alongside Dock Road. The long, narrow dock between the two ranges of mills was a basin off the East Float used by barges bringing part-loads of grain from the holds of cargo ships and passenger liners berthed elsewhere in Birkenhead and Liverpool, and grain brought by canal. Barges were also warped along the dock by hydraulic capstan, carrying internal loads between mill and warehouse. Homepride Mills were owned by Paul Brothers, and had its own dockside railway locomotive, the 1924 Hawthorne Leslie 0-4-0 saddle-tank *Homepride*, which was the pride of dockland, always smartly turned out in shiny black and red paintwork with lined panels and polished brasswork. It continued to work the mills until 1964, spending its last six years with W. J. Lee.

In 1954 a Birkenhead bus on route 12 from Charing Cross to Seacombe Ferry via Park station pauses in the middle of **DOCK ROAD, POULTON**, to drop a passenger at the iron stop flag on the graceful iron gas lamp post at the corner of Oakdale Road (right), before moving on to pass between a slow-moving horse-drawn wagon and a stationary articulated motor lorry laden with sacks of flour. The bus is a 1948 Massey-bodied Leyland Titan PD1, in service till 1961; the lorry is a 1947 Bedford. Oakdale Road was the boundary between Seacombe and Poulton, and west of this junction Dock Road entered the grim canyon of steaming, rumbling, flour-dusty mills formed by Homepride Flour Mills, continuing along the left-hand side of the road to Buchanan's Flour Mills and its Blue Cross Animal Food Mills, with their strong, sweet smell of grain.

Above The broad acres of worn granite setts (left) and rough boulder-paving (right) of **DOCK ROAD, POULTON**, take the Wallasey dock road and railways into the canyon of mills with their overhead footbridges. This 1954 view is looking east from the junction with Duke Street towards Seacombe. Lester Walter ran a workmen's canteen in a long, low shed on this side of the three-story joinery and door factory on the left. A concrete company made artificial stone in the yard beyond the joinery, and the ship propeller factory of the Manganese Bronze & Brass Company is on the left just before the bend in the road. Buchanan's Flour Mills catch the sunlight round the bend, and a majestic Art Deco extension towers in the background.

Below The funnel and wheelhouse of an old Rea steam tug rise

through the jumble of dockside paraphernalia of coal wharves around **VITTORIA CREEK**, a basin off the East Float between Vittoria Dock and Duke Street. This was the old centre of the coal trade in Birkenhead docks, where hoists tipped wagonloads of coal down chutes into ships' holds. Coal was exported as main cargo or ballast cargo, and steam coal was loaded direct to ships' bunkers or shipped as cargo to overseas coaling stations as far away as Auckland, New Zealand (where the only other Birkenhead lies just across the ferry). Even sailing ships were used in the coal trade until the 1940s.

Rea Ltd, of Monks Ferry, the main bunker coal contractors in Birkenhead, operated the wharves on Vittoria Creek and used to ship coal here in its own colliers from south Wales between the 1880s and the 1920s to augment supplies brought by train from the Denbighshire, Staffordshire, Lancashire and Yorkshire coalfields. As ships grew in size and coal-loading methods advanced from hand tips to hydraulic hoists and conveyors, the trade moved to Duke Street Wharf and Cavendish Wharf, where there was more space for railway sidings to ease congestion caused by empty coal wagons. By the 1950s Vittoria Creek was no longer used in the coal trade, and the trade itself was in terminal decline. In this 1954 picture we can still see the masts and derricks of some of the old hand-tip coal hoists standing on the side of the wharf, a railway weighbridge house on the left, and the rails of a loading spur in the foreground, at right angles to the main sidings on the left. A wagon turntable (off left) turned each wagon on to the spur, and we can just see the hydraulic capstan and part of the frame of a hydraulic wagon hoist on the wharfside.

Above Standing among the weeds on **DUKE STREET WHARF** in 1951 are *Glanmor* and *Jessie*, two of Birkenhead's quaint, elderly, privately owned dockside railway locomotives that moved freight over Mersey Docks & Harbour Board metals beyond the main-line company goods depots, shunted on the dockside, and worked private industrial sidings in dockland. Short 0-4-0 saddle-tank locomotives were used for this work because of the many tight curves in the tracks on streets and wharves and into warehouses. Most of these locomotives were second-hand from mills and collieries in other parts of Britain, owned or leased by local haulage companies under contract to the MDHB.

Glanmor is on Rea's sidings, with a birdcage spark arrester on the chimney and a shovel casually slung over the tank against the handrail. This locomotive was built by R. W. Hawthorne Leslie & Co at Newcastle-upon-Tyne in 1907, and rebuilt by Cudworth & Johnson of Wrexham in 1949. Behind is *Jessie*, built by Peckett & Sons at Bristol, also in 1907. Both engines were leased to Rea by Cudworth & Johnson, ship- and tug-owners, master porters and stevedores in bulk trades, mainly coal and iron-ore, and one of the haulage contractors to the dock board. On the right is a steam coal crane, and on the left the stern of a cargo ship at its Poulton berth on the Wallasey side of the West Float.

Left This fine glass-plate study of *Glanmor*, also on Duke Street Wharf in 1951, shows her attired in her Sunday-best tarpaulin, roped around the cab, while idle from Saturday noon till Monday morning. Its birdcage spark arrester is open after the cleaning out of the smokebox for the weekend, the shovel is laid across the buffer-beam in front of the smokebox door, and there is a range of oil cans on the running-plate between the cab shield and the sandbox. Coal was stored in the cab. Duke Street, Duke Street Bridge and Rea's store shed are in the background. *The late George Greenwood*

Over Duke Street Bridge we meet *Cyclops* again, ambling backwards along **DUKE STREET, POULTON**, in 1954 towards the bridge as it runs light between shunting duties in different parts of dockland. It is about to overtake a horse-drawn cart. Double tracks ran along the middle of Duke Street from this junction with Dock Road, Wallasey, to Corporation Road, Birkenhead, the bridge being the frontier between the two boroughs. Goods trains took their place in the normal order of road traffic along this section of Duke Street, and oncoming steam locomotives with columns of railway wagons dwarfed private cars and filed closely past the windows of buses on the joint routes 10, 11 and 12 between

Wallasey and Birkenhead. Buses on these routes were also subject to delays by ships passing the raised drawbridge and by long goods trains at Corporation Road railway crossing. On the right is the Dock Master's Office. Duke Street Bridge spanned the passage between the East Float (left) and the West Float (right). The Great Float was conceived as one big dock from Tower Road to Poulton Bridge, but Duke Street Bridge had to be built to preserve an ancient right of way of a ferry and a low-water ford across Wallasey Pool just above this point, thus dividing the Great Float into its two sections. The electric drawbridge replaced the former hydraulic swing-bridge in 1931.

Below The bows and sterns of cargo ships loomed large into the everyday comings and goings of Wallaseyans, and wharfside business was open to all who traversed the main roads to and from the island across the docks of Wallasey Pool. At **HENDERSON'S WHARF, POULTON**, looking from the north end of Duke Street in 1954, we glimpse between the Customs & Excise Office (left) and the Henderson Line warehouse (right) the Henderson steam-turbine passenger/cargo liner *Prome* (7,043 gross tons), loading for Burma at the Henderson Line berth on the West Float. P. Henderson & Company, of Glasgow, operated a scheduled service of cargo liners with passenger accommodation from this Poulton wharf to Burma via Port Said. *Prome*, built by Denny

Brothers at Dumbarton in 1937 and registered at Glasgow, had accommodation for 75 1st Class passengers and continued in service till 1962. Henderson liners had all-black funnels. In the background is the coal conveyor on Cavendish Wharf, Birkenhead.

Bottom Silhouetted against the diffused backlight of a fitful sun peeping between the sombre clouds over dockland in 1954, the coal conveyor on **CAVENDISH WHARF** loads coal aboard a collier in the West Float in the declining years of the coal trade. Beyond, on Duke Street Wharf, cranes unload iron-ore from a large freighter into railway wagons bound for steelworks in north Wales and the Black Country. On the left, Duke Street Bridge, spanning the passage between the East and West Floats, is silhouetted against the grey outline of Seacombe mills on the East Float. The wide open spaces of Duke Street Wharf and Cavendish Wharf, with their maze of railway tracks, favoured use for the export of bulk minerals and bulky machines: Welsh coal, steam coal for ships' bunkers, sand, gravel, lime and fluorspar, scrap metal, railway locomotives and carriages, lorries and cranes. Duke Street Wharf was also used for the import of metal ores – iron, tin, copper and manganese – although much of the ore trade had moved to Bidston Dock in 1951. Rea's coal conveyor on Cavendish Wharf shut down in 1961, and its Mersey bank coaling station at Monks Ferry closed in the same year.

Right The Brocklebank cargo ship *Mahsud* slips away from **CAVENDISH WHARF** bound for India with fore and aft deck cargo of steam railway locomotives from the Vulcan Foundry, Newton-le-Willows, for service on Indian Government Railways. The Ellerman ship *City of Barcelona* is loading coal at Duke Street Wharf and two other cargo ships, double-berthed astern, are unloading ores. Birkenhead docks were at their busiest in this post-war period. The bicycle propped up against stacked railway track in the right foreground still shows its wartime white-painted rear mudguard. *E. T. W. Dennis postcard*

Below A ship of the Head Line (Ulster Steamship Company) discharges grain at Joseph Rank's Ocean Flour Mills on the **WEST FLOAT**. These mills were built in 1912 on the Birkenhead side of the float west of Gill Brook Basin (left). Another basin, Rank's Creek, separated Rank's mills from W. Vernon & Sons' mill of 1898 and its post-war concrete silo to the right, on the site of the former Canada Works. Gill Brook Basin was the site of William Laird's first shipbuilding yard (1828-56). In 1954 no trace remained of this yard nor of the Canada Works (1853-89) of Thomas Brassey, the world's greatest railway contractor. This picture of Birkenhead mills was taken from the Wallasey side of the docks near Poulton, and is framed between the stern of the Ellerman cargo ship *City of Liverpool* (1949) (extreme right), the buffers of a railway wagon (left), and the mooring ropes of the next ship at the quay. The West Float, with 52 acres of water and 2½ miles of quays, also gave access to three dry docks for ship repairs, and served Spiller's Uveco cattle food mills, Calder's timber yards and a jungle of storage tanks for the United Molasses Company, Liverpool Oil Storage Company, Vacuum Oil Company and Anglo-American Oil Company. The Liverpool Victoria Rowing Club also had its boathouse on the West Float.

THE FERRIES

Six grand old steamers – of a total fleet of 11 in 1950 – plied the ferry passages across the Mersey estuary to Liverpool direct from three steamboat stations on the Cheshire bank when the seasonal New Brighton service supplemented the year-round, day-and-night services from Seacombe and Woodside. The Seacombe and Woodside ferries ran every 10 minutes in the peak periods, every 15 minutes in the off-peak and hourly through the night. New Brighton ferry ran half-hourly during daylight from Easter to October. There were regular afternoon and evening dance cruises out to sea from Liverpool and New Brighton, and occasional day cruises from Seacombe and Liverpool up the Ship Canal to Manchester and back next day. It was a brisk and well-ordered routine to ship the thousands of people who crowded the landing stages and the steamers on the intensive schedules at peak periods and holiday times.

The Mersey ferries were the biggest river passenger steamers in British waters, sturdy and robust to ride the storms of the wide river estuary and large enough to carry, variously, from 1,400 to 2,200 passengers per trip. They were navigated with great skill across the busy shipping lanes in the night and in fog and storm, and the 150-foot-long steamers (with no bow-thrusters) were swung round against the surge and swell of the 6-knot current to berth at Liverpool stage with only 5 feet between them. The world's first commercial shore-based radar station, installed in Seacombe Ferry clock tower in 1947, guided both Wallasey and Birkenhead ferries across the river in the densest fog.

The ferries were the most popular way to cross the river, against the railway and road tunnels. The fresh air and close-up views of world shipping were a daily tonic for the bowler-hat-and-briefcase brigade of businessmen who paraded two and three abreast counter-clockwise around the promenade decks of the steamers on the three-quarter-mile passages from Woodside and Seacombe in the peak periods. On Sunday mornings the Woodside steamers conveyed hundreds of cyclists on their way from Liverpool to Wirral and Wales and back again in the evening. In the Easter and summer holidays the 2¼-mile ferry trip down river to New Brighton was like a sea cruise in itself for the thousands of day-trippers from Liverpool heading for the sands and fairground. Wallasey Ferries also offered afternoon and evening dance cruises from Liverpool and New Brighton 11 miles out to sea to the Bar Lightship.

This was the picture in the post-war period from 1945 till passenger figures, which peaked in 1948-49, gradually declined during the 1950s. The Woodside night ferry service ended in 1956 and the Seacombe night ferry followed in 1962. The New Brighton service closed in 1971, hastened by siltation of the berth and storm damage to the pier.

The Mersey ferries were Merseysiders' own little ships. For those who were not seamen they were probably the only ships on which they ever sailed, apart, perhaps, from the occasional excursion to Llandudno or Douglas. Those excursions were expensive – 12s 6d to Llandudno adult return in 1950, when the average family lived on less than £7 a week. They were thus a rare treat, experienced only once or twice in a lifetime, while it only cost us a few pennies to cross the Mersey by ferry. It only cost me, as a boy, 1d on the Woodside Ferry – the best pennyworth in Britain. Trippers could go from Liverpool to New Brighton for 1 shilling return, or a dance cruise down the river to the sea for half-a-crown (2s 6d). The ferries were the best recreation on Merseyside. They were an essential part of our everyday life on the Cheshire bank and were etched into our psyche; every man and boy had his own favourite ferry steamer.

FROM SAIL TO STEAM

Steam ferries were the most important factor in the history and development of Birkenhead and Wallasey. There are no written records of when the early ferries began because they were an informal, ad hoc provision by local boatmen ferrying travellers, horses and farm produce in large rowing boats with auxiliary sails and landing on the shore; passengers were lifted ashore on the backs of the ferrymen. The ferries were already in being when they were mentioned in the earliest extant records: Woodside in 1282, Seacombe in 1330, Tranmere in 1541, Rock Ferry in 1660 and New Ferry in 1774.

We do know that a Royal charter of 1330 granted the monks of Birkenhead Priory the legal, exclusive rights to operate Woodside Ferry and to charge tolls, and that the Crown, which owned the foreshore, leased the rights of Seacombe Ferry to William Bromley in 1541 and Tranmere Ferry to John Poole in 1586. The monks also started a ferry across Wallasey Pool to Limekiln Lane, Poulton, in the 14th century to reach their lands in Wallasey. Although the ferries put the Wirral peninsula on the road map between Chester and Liverpool, it was still entirely rural until the 1820s and '30s brought steam ferries. Wealthy Liverpool merchants and professional gentlemen came to escape from the bustle and slums of the city to establish the initial, salubrious, villa colonies at Birkenhead from 1820, New Brighton from 1834 and Rock Ferry from 1836. Rock Ferry and New Ferry gave their names to the districts they created and served.

The first steamship on the Mersey was on the Liverpool-Runcorn ferry in 1815. Steam ferries followed to Ellesmere Port and Eastham in 1816, Tranmere in 1817, Birkenhead (Abbey Street) in 1820, Woodside and Seacombe in 1822, New Ferry in 1826, Egremont in 1830, Rock Ferry in 1832, New Brighton in 1834, and Monks Ferry in 1838. The services to Birkenhead, Monks Ferry, Egremont and New Brighton started with steam.

Horse-drawn coaches plied between Tranmere Ferry and Parkgate to connect with ferries across the firth of Dee to Flint and Bagillt, and the first steam ferry on the Dee appeared on the Bagillt service in 1817, the same year as at Tranmere. This was one way passengers travelled between Liverpool and North Wales from the 1780s till the completion of the railway link via Chester in 1848. The Parkgate coaches terminated at Tranmere Ferry till 1844, then Birkenhead Ferry till 1850, and Rock Ferry till 1866, when the railway opened from Hooton to Parkgate. You could also go to Wales via Eastham Ferry and Queen's Ferry.

The first Tranmere steamer, the 63-foot 75-ton PS Ætna, had one paddle wheel between two wooden hulls, decked right across, which made it easier to load horse-drawn vehicles than on conventional side-wheel paddle-steamers. It remained in service for 15 years till 1832. The first New Brighton steamer, the 104-foot 92-ton Sir John Moore, seemed diminutive enough on the more exposed New Brighton passage, having a beam of only 16ft 7in (across the deck and bulwarks), but this steamer was second-hand and had served for seven years as an Irish mail steamer plying between Glasgow and Dun Laoghaire. A fine model of this ferry steamer in a glass case graced Seacombe Ferry tollhouse, and is now in the Earlston Reference Library in Upper Brighton.

Sir John Moore was typical of the long-funnelled, wooden-hulled, open-decked paddle-steamers of the period, with a railed, open bridge spanning the paddle boxes. The only shelter was a small, ill-ventilated saloon below deck next to the engine room. The pioneer steamers carried a sail rig on the mast in case of engine failure, and boilers were liable to explode. Such were the ferries that plied across the Mersey in the 1820s, '30s and '40s. Ferry passengers had to share the decks with goods, horses, carts, carriages, livestock and sacks of farm produce. Iron-hulled paddle-steamers arrived at Woodside and Egremont in 1836, but the transition from sail to steam was piecemeal; wooden sailing ferries continued for 31 years into the steam era on the Mersey ferries. New Ferry had a steamer from 1826 but was the last Mersey ferry to use sail, till 1846.

PIERS AND STAGES

My early interest in Merseyside local history was aroused by drawings, paintings and engravings of the quaint ferry landing places in rustic settings along the Cheshire bank in the late 18th and early 19th centuries. The pioneer steamers landed at stone slipways, like the one that survives at Rock Ferry, dated 1820, but Egremont Ferry opened in 1830 with second-hand paddle-steamers plying from a short 200-foot wooden pier at high water only, and New Brighton Ferry opened in 1834 with a rickety-looking wooden pier, 500 feet long, with sheds on deck, guyed up with chains staked to the bedrock just under the sand.

In 1835-36 the three Wallasey ferries, under separate ownership, introduced 'run-out' stages to reach the steamers at low water. The one at New Brighton was a floating stage (which might have been a hulk or barge) pulled out on the ebb tide by the departing steamer and hauled up on the flow tide by a horse-powered windlass fixed to the bedrock. At Seacombe a movable wooden pier was mounted on an inclined undercarriage that ran on rails down the stone slipway under its own weight and was hauled up by a steam engine on the stage. In 1858 a stationary steam engine was installed in a brick engine-house with a chimney at the top of the slipway and hauled up the stage by chain. Egremont had a stationary steam engine and a stone slipway built under the pier to carry the railbound extension. In 1850-56 Egremont pier was extended to 238 feet and the stage runway to 798 feet, with a larger winding engine, and the ferry company built a small, pioneer gasworks to light the ferry approach and supply gas to holders in two gas-lit steamers.

The mid-19th century was a time of intense rivalry, with nine ferry services across the Mersey to Liverpool between New Ferry and New Brighton. This was the period of the short-lived Monks Ferry, from a stone slipway at the end of Ivy Street, Birkenhead, which in our own time was Monks Ferry coaling station for tugs and coasters. Monks Ferry was near the priory ruins, but it was not the ferry passage worked by the monks of Birkenhead. They worked the ferry from Woodside, the shortest and oldest continuous ferry passage across the Mersey, where the roads from Chester and Hoylake converged. The monks worked the ferry from the 13th century till the priory closed in 1536, when the ferry rights passed first to the Crown then to successive lords of the manor of Birkenhead. Monks Ferry operated from 1838 to 1840, then again from 1842 to 1878 as a railway passenger ferry when Monks Ferry was the railhead for Birkenhead; the railway was diverted to Woodside Ferry in 1878.

The making of the Mersey ferries resulted from the transition to public ownership. Liverpool Corporation acquired Birkenhead Ferry in 1841, the first municipal transport operation in Britain.

The following year Monks Ferry and Woodside Ferry were leased to the Birkenhead Improvement Commissioners, who bought Woodside Ferry in 1860 but surrendered the lease of Monks Ferry back to the owning railway company in 1862. Wallasey Local Board of Health bought the ferry rights at Seacombe, Egremont and New Brighton in 1861. The regular, reliable services, cheap tolls, floating landing stages, saloon steamers and screw-steamers, and separate goods ferries at Woodside and Seacombe, developed under municipal enterprise, popularised the ferry services, drew great crowds of passengers to the Woodside, Seacombe and New Brighton services, and led to the rapid urban development of Birkenhead and Wallasey in the second half of the 19th century.

Tolls were cut to 1d on the shorter ferry passages from 1848. All-night ferry services began from Woodside in 1849 and from Seacombe in 1880. To cater for the maximum 31ft 6in tidal range in the Mersey, floating landing stages with hinged bridges springing from the new river wall were commissioned at Woodside in 1862 and Seacombe in 1880, and from a new 600-foot-long iron pier at New Brighton in 1867. Still being run by private enterprise, New Ferry was provided with an 850-foot iron pier in 1865, and Tranmere Ferry with a 750-foot iron pier in 1877, both with floating stages. New Ferry and New Brighton piers were built to the same design by James Brunlees. Other landings at Rock Ferry, Birkenhead Ferry and Monks Ferry were still stone slipways.

The new ferry landing place at Woodside was created by landfill from the river bank at the foot of the slope below the Woodside Hotel, where Chester Street meets Hamilton Street, embedding the massive 700-foot-long stone pier of 1835 with its twin slipways under the new ferry approach, and building a river wall to project the new landing stage into deeper water.

This landing stage (1862-1985) was 800 feet long and 80 feet wide, secured to the river wall by chains, booms, a passenger bridge, a cattle bridge and a floating road. The south end of the stage was used by passenger and goods ferries, and the north end was owned by Mersey Docks & Harbour Board for landing cattle at the lairage and for coaling tugs. The ferry terminal buildings on the stage and the wall were erected in 1863-64. The lighthouse that stood on the end of the 1835 jetty still stands on the river wall beside the colonnaded, wooden tollhouse of 1864.

The floating road, 670 feet long, springing from the old shoreline at the foot of Hamilton Street, was laid down a gap between the ferry approach and the cattle lairage in 1865-68 to carry vehicles down to the goods ferry. This gap was part of the former Woodside Basin, where ferries landed at temporary slipways during the reclamation and construction. When Woodside Landing Stage was replaced in 1985 it was the oldest floating structure in the world.

Seacombe Ferry had its first floating stage in 1876, a temporary, second-hand one, with a short wooden pier and bridges in a disused shipyard on the docks side of the ferry slip, while reclamation in 1876-80 lined up the river wall with the dock wall, embedded the 1835 stone slipway under a new ferry approach, Victoria Place, and provided a permanent floating landing stage connected by a passenger bridge. Instead of a floating road, Seacombe Ferry had a hinged goods bridge for use at high water, and an iron pier with two goods lifts to the stage for use at low water.

The dock railway along Birkenhead Road brought coal direct to the ferry. Rails, with wagon turntables, were laid into the decks of the pier, the lifts and landing stage and the first goods ferry, the paddle-steamer *Sunflower* of 1879, to ship railway goods wagons across the Mersey to Liverpool, but the rails were never used because the Dock Board made no railway connection on the Liverpool side. The lifts, wagon capstans and the goods and passenger gangways were powered by a hydraulic engine housed in an ornate brick clock tower next to the tollhouse.

Landing places on the Liverpool side were at steps, slipways and tidal basins along the river wall and the outer walls of the impounded docks. Eighteenth-century drawings show primitive, wooden, ferry piers at the foot of Water Street and Hanover Street, but they were shortly replaced by dock construction. The first floating stage was at Seacombe Ferry Basin off Prince's Dock in 1842. The first George's Landing Stage, 508 feet long, was built off George's Dock wall in 1847. Prince's Stage was a separate stage sited off Prince's Dock in 1858 for Irish Sea ferries and ocean liners. A new

George's Stage, 600 feet, was installed in 1874-76, complete with a floating road for goods ferry traffic. A new Prince's Stage was joined on to the north end of George's Stage in 1896. At a combined 2,478 feet, Liverpool Landing Stage was the largest floating structure in the world – and still to be extended. It lasted till 1975.

SALOON STEAMERS

The first steamers with saloons at deck level were the paddlers *Cheshire* (150 feet, 421 tons) at Woodside and *Heatherbell* (160 feet, 205 tons) at Seacombe in 1863. They were the forerunners of the next generation of Mersey ferries: double-ended vessels with twin, upright funnels, saloons along the middle of the main deck, rounded at each end, with a broad walkway all round, stairs to the promenade decks on top, and two gangway gates in the bulwarks on each side.

The improved landing facilities and saloon paddle-steamers brought big business to Woodside Ferry, which, on its own, carried double the loadings of the three Wallasey ferries to the still growing townships of Seacombe, Egremont and New Brighton. The number of passengers passing through Woodside tollhouse topped the 10 million mark from 1873 to 1876 and again from 1880 to 1886, peaking at 12,036,958 in 1884. The opening of the Mersey Railway in 1886 halved the number of ferry passengers to and from Birkenhead and the figures did not rise to this level again till the 1920s. The under-river railway from Liverpool to Birkenhead made no impression on the patronage of Wallasey Ferries, which continued to rise steadily; from 1886 Wallasey's passengers outnumbered those of Birkenhead.

The first screw-steamers appeared on the goods ferries in 1879-82, but it was 1885 before they appeared in passenger service, with the Wallasey sisters *Crocus* and *Snowdrop* (130 feet, 300 tons). They were the first ferries licensed to carry more than 1,000 passengers – 1,303, in fact – and the last double-enders to be built, thus having twin screws at both ends. The first screw-steamer at Woodside, *Cheshire* (137 feet, 380 tons) in 1889 represented the reversion to single-ended, single-funnelled passenger ferries. *Crocus*, *Snowdrop* and *Cheshire* were also the first steel-hulled Mersey ferries. The double-enders survived on passenger service at Woodside till 1894 and at Wallasey till 1909. After *Crocus* and *Snowdrop*, Wallasey built three more paddlers, and the PS *John Herron* of 1896 was the last paddle ferry on the Mersey when it left in 1916.

GOODS FERRIES

Passenger and goods services were separated at Woodside from 1846, when two Mersey flats (sailing barges) were used to ship goods across the river, followed by relegated passenger steamers, which, with their open decks, did not need much conversion to carry goods. They used the south slipway on Woodside jetty while passenger steamers used the north slipway. When the new stage opened in 1862, the goods ferries used the cattle bridge till the floating road opened in 1868.

The separation of goods at Seacombe began with the relegated passenger steamer *Elizabeth* in 1862 for one year. For the next 17 years passenger steamers carried only goods at certain times, and were augmented by a barge, towed behind passenger steamers, carrying bricks, cement, coal and hay to Seacombe, Egremont and New Brighton. Further separation of goods from passengers at Seacombe was achieved by loading goods at the old earth and stone slipway of 1815, just south of the 1835 slipway and run-out stage used by passengers.

Goods ferries on the Mersey were known as 'luggage boats', and carried unaccompanied luggage, hampers, parcels, boxes, barrels, sacks, livestock and deadstock. A list of Wallasey tolls in 1867 included corpses, coffins, chimney pots, fire grates, ice, mussels and pigs (alive or dead). The goods ferries were also vehicular ferries, and most of the traffic came in hand-carts and horse-drawn carts and wagons, which formed long queues at the ferry approaches on both sides of the river, as the service was confined to the higher states of the tide, when the horses could negotiate the sloping bridge at George's Stage, Liverpool.

The opening of the 560-foot floating road on George's Stage in 1876, followed by the separation of goods at Seacombe with the remodelling of the ferry terminus in 1880 and the first purpose-built goods steamers at Woodside in 1879 and

Seacombe in 1880, really opened up the goods services and got the long queues moving on both sides of the river.

The first screw-drive ferry steamers appeared on the goods services. They were bluff-bowed double-enders with clear decks and twin screws at both ends: the Woodside sisters *Oxton* and *Bebington* (130 feet, 430 tons) in 1879 and '80, and the similar Seacombe goods ferry *Wallasey* (140 feet, 459 tons) in 1882. These double-twin-screw steamers set a design standard for the goods ferries till the services ended in the 1940s.

MUNICIPAL DEVELOPMENTS

Meanwhile, Liverpool Corporation had backed a loser on the Birkenhead Ferry. The Birkenhead Hotel closed in 1850 and the three iron paddle-steamers of 1848-49 were operated by lessees from 1851. The ferry lost business to its neighbours at Tranmere, Monks Ferry and Woodside, and closed in 1870. Birkenhead became a borough in 1877, and Birkenhead Corporation inherited Woodside Ferry from the Improvement Commissioners. Wallasey became an urban district in 1894, and the District Council acquired the Seacombe, Egremont and New Brighton ferries from the Local Board.

Birkenhead Corporation took over Rock Ferry and New Ferry in 1897, introducing saloon screw-steamers. New Ferry already had a pier and floating stage, and the Corporation built a 780-foot iron pier and floating stage at Rock Ferry, opened in 1899. Tranmere Ferry, with its pier and floating stage of 1877, still privately owned, operated intermittently and closed finally in 1904. Wallasey became a borough in 1910, when Wallasey Corporation took over the ferries from the UDC.

Birkenhead and Wallasey Corporations now each worked two ferry services from three landing places, their intensive 24-hour passenger and goods ferries working the shortest passages from Woodside and Seacombe. Their secondary ferries up-river and down-river of the Mersey narrows were combined services, New Ferry steamers calling at Rock Ferry, and New Brighton steamers calling at Egremont.

The turn of the century saw the final development of the passenger ferries on the

Mersey, with twin-screw steamers that set design standards for their respective fleets for the next 50 years: the Birkenhead ferry *Lancashire* (150 feet, 469 tons) of 1899 and the Wallasey ferry *Rose* (155 feet, 514 tons) of 1900, with a bridge added in 1901, spanning the promenade deck.

Egremont Ferry station was entirely rebuilt in 1908-09 with a new tollhouse and a conventional pier with a bridge to a floating stage, replaced by a larger stage in 1929. George's Stage at Liverpool was extended south by 55 feet in 1922 to provide a second berth for Woodside goods steamers. There were three or four goods ferries on the Woodside service simultaneously, but only one from Seacombe. The combined Liverpool Landing Stage was now 2,533 feet, or nearly half a mile, long, with berths for ferries to Eastham, Rock Ferry/New Ferry, Woodside, Seacombe and Egremont/New Brighton.

In 1926 the goods pier and hydraulic lifts at Seacombe were replaced by a three-lane floating road, 590 feet long, to a new stage, 485 feet long with three berths, and in 1930-33 the ferry buildings were replaced with new workshops, tollhouse, offices, bus station and indoor car park. These were impressively built in the grand neo-classical style of the period in red brick and Portland stone with Tuscan colonnades and Art Deco wooden kiosks in the spacious arrival and departure booking halls (all Mersey ferry tolls both ways being paid on the Cheshire bank).

The Corporation also made improvements to New Brighton ferry pier with a new landing stage (242 feet by 45 feet) in 1921, and in the winter of 1935-36 the ferry closed for structural strengthening of the pier with a wider deck and a new Art Deco tollhouse halfway along.

The most famous Mersey ferry steamers in history, the Wallasey sisters *Iris* and *Daffodil*, built in 1906, were both 152 feet and 465 tons and the first Mersey ferries with full-width promenade decks. They became *Royal Iris* and *Royal Daffodil* after taking part as troopships in the Royal Navy blockade of Zeebrugge harbour, the entrance to a German submarine base at Brugge, in 1918. They were chosen for working in minefields because of their double hulls and shallow draught. They were armour-plated for the operation, but were damaged by shells and bullets with flooded engine rooms,

and there were many casualties on board the *Iris*. Both ships were restored by ferry staff and continued in service till 1931 and 1934 respectively.

Royal Iris started regular summer holiday dance cruises from New Brighton and Liverpool in 1924, plying up-river to Eastham or down-river to the Mersey Bar, with refreshments and a dance band on the promenade deck. She was succeeded as a cruise steamer in turn by *Royal Daffodil* in 1932 and *Francis Storey* in 1934. Wallasey Ferries had also run cruises up the Manchester Ship Canal since its opening in 1894.

The inter-war years were the heyday of the Mersey ferries, and passenger loadings did not reflect the trade slump and unemployment. From 1917-18 to 1940-41 Woodside Ferry loadings were consistently in excess of 10 million, peaking in 1926-27 with 14,093,135. Trippers on the New Brighton Ferry peaked in the last year of the war, 1917-18, with 6,951,463, and fluctuated above the 3 million mark until 1936. Seacombe Ferry, the busiest of the three, carried a peak 21,932,176 passengers in 1920-21, and more than 20,000,000 a year from 1925 to 1934.

CLOSURES

The last of the privately owned ferries, Eastham, with its three saloon paddle-steamers *Pearl*, *Ruby* and *Sapphire* of 1897-98 plying from a short, iron pier and floating stage, closed in 1929, as Eastham had ceased to be a riverside resort. New Ferry and Egremont Ferry were both closed by ships colliding with the piers when both were losing money. A Dutch coaster wrecked the outer end of New Ferry pier in fog in 1922, and the service was curtailed at Rock Ferry. In 1932 a drifting oil tanker wrecked Egremont pier head and bridge, but the damage was repaired and the service resumed in 1933. From the closure of New Brighton pier for structural work in the winter of 1935-36, the ferry service to Egremont and New Brighton was reduced to a seasonal service only. In 1939 Rock Ferry was closed as uneconomic, and Egremont Ferry was suspended for the Second World War, never to re-open. The demolition of Egremont pier by a drifting coaster in 1941 spelled the end of service there.

The Edwardian era had ushered in the motor vehicle, which began to infiltrate the ranks of the horse-drawn vehicles on the goods ferries. After the First World War the increase in motor cars, vans and lorries caused long queues to form again at the floating roads on both sides of the river. The Mersey road tunnel between Birkenhead and Liverpool opened in 1934, siphoning off most of the goods ferry traffic, but hand-carts, horse-wagons, steam-lorries and dangerous loads were banned from the tunnel. Woodside goods ferry continued till 1941, when both Birkenhead goods steamers and one of Wallasey's goods steamers were requisitioned for war service and converted to floating cranes on the Mersey.

Seacombe goods ferry was busy through the war but still lost money. The Great Western Railway continued to use it to link up with its railless receiving depots in Liverpool because the railway company was still using horse-drawn vans and wagons for goods and luggage feeder services. The GWR, which normally used Woodside goods ferry, had two contract periods to use Seacombe goods ferry instead, from 1918 to 1923 and again from 1937 to 1947. So little traffic was using the goods ferry after the war that, when the railway contract expired in 1947, the ferry closed. Wallasey's DTSS *Perch Rock* (144 feet, 766 tons) of 1929 was the last Mersey goods ferry.

WAR AND AFTER

Woodside and Seacombe ferries steamed on as normal through the Second World War, although service was suspended when mines were dropped in the river till they were cleared by minesweepers. Spare passenger ferries were often called on to act as tenders to troopships in Crosby Channel and mid-river when Prince's Landing Stage was busy. The requisitioned goods ferries were refitted as floating cranes to unload American aircraft kits from ships in mid-river for assembly at Speke; a total of 11,000 aircraft were transhipped this way. In the air raids of 1940-41 goods ferries were also used to raise smoke screens over Merseyside and as fire-fighting vessels in the docks, while Wallasey's TSS *Royal Daffodil II* of 1934 stood by to evacuate troopships anchored in mid-river if necessary.

In the 1941 May blitz two Birkenhead ferries,

Claughton of 1931 and *Bidston* of 1933, were damaged by bomb blast and flying debris while in service, and Wallasey's *Royal Daffodil II* was sunk by a bomb while berthed off-service at Seacombe stage one night. The direct hit smashed her starboard engine, but her crew survived and the ship was raised by ferry staff in 1942 and restored to service in 1943. Wallasey's *J. Farley* and *Francis Storey* of 1922 were commissioned by the Admiralty to fit anti-torpedo nets to merchant ships in the Western Approaches. *Francis Storey* worked in Liverpool Bay and *J. Farley* in Milford Haven and the Firth of Clyde, with their Wallasey captains and crews under Naval command. The year 1941-42 was the low point in the fortunes of the Mersey ferries, when the number of passengers on both the Birkenhead and Wallasey ferries dropped to half their peak levels of the 1920s.

To relieve the gloom of war, the Birkenhead ferry *Hinderton* of 1925 ran occasional river cruises up to Eastham and down to the Mersey Bar in Liverpool Bay from 1942 to 1946. When war was over, VE and VJ celebration dance cruises on *Royal Daffodil II* started the post-war afternoon and evening cruise programme from Liverpool and New Brighton out to the Mersey Bar at least three days a week; these were 2-hour cruises with a dance band, buffet, licensed bar and a commentary by the captain on the river scene. *J. Farley* ran irregular day excursions up and down the Manchester Ship Canal.

The Mersey ferries emerged from war into their post-war heyday with Birkenhead Corporation operating Woodside Ferry and Wallasey Corporation operating from Seacombe and New Brighton. Rock Ferry and Egremont Ferry were not part of the revival. Rock Ferry pier and stage remained open for tugmen, fishermen and yachtsmen till 1957, and the shipwrecked ruins of Egremont pier were removed in 1946 and the old run-out slipway in 1947-48. Birkenhead had a fleet of four passenger steamers built in 1925-33, and Wallasey had six passenger steamers dating from 1922-34. Two steamers worked each service while the others were kept in steam on stand-by or docked for servicing, repairs or refit. Wallasey also had one former goods ferry, the DTSS *Perch Rock* of 1929, now with buoyant seats on the deck; she helped with the New Brighton crowds on busy holidays from 1948 to 1953.

This was the Indian summer of the Mersey ferries. Passenger figures rose again to new peaks of 16,744,401 on the Seacombe Ferry and 4,299,193 on the New Brighton Ferry in 1947-48, with 11,400,795 on the Woodside Ferry in 1948-49. Wallasey Ferries made a trading loss from 1948-49 onwards. Ferry passengers stabilised around 1950 and cruising peaked in 1951-52 with 326,750 passengers, but then patronage slowly began to decline through the 1950s. During this decade the number of Wallasey ferry passengers halved from 19,834,121 in 1949-50 to 9,827,443 in 1959-60. Over the same period Birkenhead ferry passenger numbers declined from 11,098,928 to 6,985,000. This was the economic context in which the hourly night ferries stopped running at Woodside in 1956 and from Seacombe in 1962. In 1971, the last year of the New Brighton Ferry, the figures for both the Wallasey ferries were down to 3,306,522. Birkenhead's figures dropped below the 1 million mark in 1982.

BIRKENHEAD FERRIES, 1950

The fresh, salty wind off the Mersey hit you in the face as you walked over the brow of Chester Street or Hamilton Street, Birkenhead, and down the slope of the river bank by the Woodside Hotel. The heart quickened as you saw the broad, brown, turgid, tearing tideway and the ferry steamer coming into the landing stage. Hazy sunlight filtered through the pall of thin cloud and smoke over Merseyside and sparkled on the water. The noble trinity of buildings on Liverpool Pier Head stood out like a mirage on the satanic, industrial Lancashire skyline, frontier of the Northern province, half a mile across the boundary river. The soot-black Royal Liver Building dominated the scene with its twin clock towers, fore and aft, and the deep, sonorous chimes sounded over the estuary towns on a still night, but you had to be downwind to hear them on a windy day.

The words 'FERRY TO LIVERPOOL', presumably for the information of aeronauts, were painted in large white letters along the roof of the Woodside ferry tollhouse of 1864, a long wooden shed on stout, ornate iron pillars, entered under an even longer iron colonnade. From the railway station and bus station passengers continually filed into the ferry booking hall with its row of octagonal wooden tollbooths, some of them leaning slightly with subsidence. We dropped our bronze coins on the brass plate of the cash desk (I paid 1d and adults 2½d from 1949 to 1955) and clicked through the turnstiles. We ran through the concourse and down the slope of the hinged bridge to the floating stage if the ferry steamer was already in, our footsteps echoing under the glazed barrel-vault of the bridge and the multi-barrelled wooden roof of the landing stage. Arrival and departure was a brisk business, all over in a few minutes in the peak periods, but there was an 8-minute lay-over in the off-peak. If the two ferries on service were on passage, then we could take our time.

Waiting passengers were corralled in a pen on the stage at the foot of the bridge (to prevent arrivals making a round trip without paying) and from there all eyes were on the approaching steamer, ploughing across the swift river and easing into the stage. There was also a large waiting room on the south-west corner of the stage, with continuous wooden seating around the panelled wooden walls and pairs of windows giving views of the shipping up-river, the dry docks at Woodside and the shipyards at Tranmere. The 800-foot-long stage, dating from 1862, moved gently on the swell. A few tugs were usually tied up at the north end of the stage, on which stood neat rows of sacks of coal. The stage was still used as a bunkering station for Birkenhead Ferries and tugs and for disembarking cattle on the hoof for the lairage.

The ferries always landed into the tide as an aircraft lands into the wind. On the ebb tide the ferry came on a slight course to starboard almost straight into its berth at Woodside, but on a flow tide it swung round through about 125 degrees up-river of the stage, throwing up waves and spray on a rough day, to make its approach from the opposite direction on a course to port. (The reverse happened at Seacombe, which was down-river of Liverpool.) The steamer loomed large as it came alongside the stage, its superstructure rising above the stage roof, and it looked as if it was on a collision course with the stage till, with only yards to go, the engines went into reverse, creating foam under each side of the vessel, and, with skilful use of the screws, the current and ropes, the steamer berthed gently against the giant rubber tyres hung along the front of the timber stage. Rarely did the steamers overshoot and have to make a second attempt at berthing.

There was a rumble as the fore and aft sliding gates in the bulwarks were rolled aside, then a clink of light iron chains as the stagehands unshackled the two drawbridge gangways mounted on turntables on the stage. The gangways were balanced with weights in an upright position, so the stagehands pushed them outwards then leaped upon them as they were poised at 45 degrees, holding the handrails, to bring them down on to the deck of the steamer with a loud clack of wood on wood. The crowds trooped off, up to four abreast, foot passengers first, cyclists last. The waiting passengers were then released from the pen and clattered across the two wooden gangways on to the steamer's main deck.

It was on the point of crossing the drawbridges on to the ferry steamer – at Woodside, Liverpool or Seacombe – that the salty smell of the Mersey was at its strongest as it swirled underneath at 6 knots. If the tide was ebbing, the salty tang was mixed with the equally refreshing smell of freshwater and sometimes a whiff of raw sewage. The steamer itself contributed its own aroma of coal smoke mixed with steam and cylinder oil. This, for me, was the smell of Merseyside, and the total mixture was a tonic.

The dark-brown, varnished wooden saloons on the main deck – forward, middle and aft – were divided by two wide aisles across the deck between the fore and aft gangway gates on each side of the ship and surrounded by a broad walkway all the way round the bulwarks under the shelter of the overhang of the promenade deck above. A stout timber coping rail ran around the top the bulwarks with brass ends at the gangway gates. Here we could watch the deckhands working the ropes and watch the turbulence and foam churned up by the twin screws at the stern. Here we could also catch the sounds of the engine room telegraph bell down the engineers' companionway, and even see the engines and stokers through the clerestory lights under the longitudinal bench seats backing on to the saloon.

Four broad stairways, two forward and two aft, with brass handrails led us up from the gangway gates, beside the fore and aft saloons, to the promenade deck, which covered the full length and width of the ship. There was no shelter up here, but these Birkenhead steamers had a steel framework for a canvas awning abaft the funnel that I never saw used and was removed about 1955. Like a seaside promenade the deck was bordered by iron handrails, painted white and hung with red-and-white lifebelts, and abaft the funnel stood what looked like two Punch & Judy stands...

The clear top deck gave us a 360-degree panorama of the Mersey scene and a grandstand view of the shipping, interrupted only by the funnel, the wheelhouse, the port and starboard telegraph boxes, which stood on deck, and two rectangular wooden cabinets, like Punch & Judy stands, that were the engine room ventilator cowls, spaced out in line abaft the funnel. I expected Mr Punch to pop out of these cowls at any time for a deck show, but, if he did, I never saw him. Much more interesting to me were the sounds of the engine room – its telegraph bell and stokers shovelling coal into the boiler furnaces – that emanated from these strange cowls.

The saloons, wheelhouse, telegraph boxes, ventilator cowls and the Spartan seating indoors and outdoors were all in stained or painted dark-brown varnished woodwork. The back-to-back seats amidships on the top deck were festooned with rope loops and wooden hand-grips, and were designed to float if the ship sank. A lifeboat sat at the back of the top deck under twin derricks. This was the basic general arrangement of the Mersey ferry steamers of the first half of the 20th century, only slightly modified in the diesel vessels of the second half-century.

As I stood on the promenade deck of the Woodside Ferry for the first time at the age of 11, having just arrived by train from southern England on a sunny, summer's afternoon in 1949, I was overwhelmed not only by the vastness and volume of the river, the shipping and the buildings of Liverpool, but also I had never been on a river steamer as large as this. It dwarfed the Salter Brothers steamers I had known on the Thames below Oxford, but I suppose they were only steam launches; this was a real ship, although on Merseyside it was only one of the little ships of the river like the tugs and dredgers and salvage vessels. The ferries were usually referred to locally as 'boats'.

To put things in proportion, the four Birkenhead Corporation Ferries of that period, *Hinderton*, *Thurstaston*, *Claughton* and *Bidston*, though built over a period from 1925 to 1933, were all of a standard design, 150 feet long, 41 feet wide, 484-487 tons, and licensed to carry 1,433 passengers. Wallasey Corporation Ferries, down-river, were bigger still.

The brass bell on the wheelhouse clanged to hasten the late runners. The gangways were raised and as the ropes were cast off there was a hoarse blast on the brass, organ-pipe, trombone steam-whistle. With the distant ring of the engine room telegraph, the screws began to thresh the water against the landing stage and we were off into adventure across the Mersey, heading for the fantasy that was Liverpool. It was a three-quarter-mile passage diagonally across the river to Liverpool and the trip took 7 minutes.

On a hazy day the ferry appeared to ply a passage across a strait between two seas. Indeed, the visitor could be forgiven for looking up-river and thinking he was looking out to sea because the Mersey widens to 3 miles in its upper estuary between Ellesmere Port and Oglet and the great hills of Delamere Forest would be lost in the haze with the silhouettes of ocean-going cargo ships on their way to and from Bromborough, Garston and the Manchester Ship Canal. In the opposite direction the river mouth was only a mile wide between New Brighton and Bootle.

Now well under way, the steamer cut through the water fringed in surf with black smoke billowing from the tall funnel and a flock of wheeling gulls overhead and in its wake. Birkenhead Ferries were the fastest on the river, being slimmer and more like steam yachts than their beamy Wallasey cousins and seemingly more manoeuvrable.

Birkenhead steamers also cut a rather anachronistic but distinctive figure on the river, with their tall funnels in faded Indian red with broad black bands top and bottom, their navigation boxes standing on the deck, their Punch & Judy box ventilators, their rope fenders hanging over the bulwarks against the rubbing strake like tugs, and their names in cursive script on the bows. They had an old-fashioned love of fresh air with their completely open promenade decks and draughty aisles and seating areas around the main deck saloons. All four Birkenhead ferries were built locally by Cammell, Laird at Tranmere, and the Corporation conservatively stuck to coal-fired steamers to the end of the 1950s.

As we crossed the busy shipping lanes we were treated to close-up views of a constant procession to and fro of smoking tugs, cargo ships, barges, dredgers and, occasionally, a floating crane, then, as we drew nearer Liverpool Landing Stage, the arrival and departure of the Seacombe and New Brighton ferries, with the North Wales and Isle of Man steamers and one or two ocean liners berthed at the stage in the background.

The mirage of Liverpool waterfront materialised as a reality, looking like a cross between New Delhi and New York in the 1930s, with canyons of tall and noble office buildings reaching through the city centre, spanned by the girders of the Overhead Railway just behind the waterfront. The slow-moving mass of matt-black and dark-green on George's Pier Head above the landing stage transpired to be the city tram terminus with war-weary and soot-stained double-deckers shunting and shuffling around the three terminal loops on the river wall at the top of the bridges down to the landing stage.

As we steamed in to our berth at the stage, the captain or mate, smartly dressed in his officer's uniform, left the wheelhouse for the nearside telegraph box, the engines went into reverse and the forward deckhand threw out a pilot line to a stagehand with a lean, weather-beaten face and a dark-blue guernsey. The stagehand hauled in the noose of the hefty mooring rope and heaved it over a bollard on the stage. The engine room telegraph rang out orders for intermittent use of forward and reverse engines on port or starboard screws and, as the back end of the steamer closed with the stage, the aft deckhand lassoed a bollard on it with the big mooring rope and both deckhands quickly tightened the fore and aft ropes in figures of eight around the twin bollards in the bulwarks. The gangway gates rumbled aside, the passengers dutifully formed up behind the brass strips in the deck opposite the gangway gates and, as the gangways touched down on the brass strips, ready feet tramped across the wooden drawbridge on to the stage and up the barrel-roofed bridges to the trams.

In the off-peak, George's and Prince's Landing Stages were Liverpool's promenade, where men and boys spotted ships and elderly women fed the pigeons and gulls. However, there was no room for promenading on George's Stage in the peak periods when the ferries shipped crowds in thousands from Woodside and Seacombe after breakfast to work in Liverpool, and back again for tea – nor on bank holidays, when anything up to 100,000 people made the trip to New Brighton. At peak times three gangways were used at each ferry berth, at Liverpool, Woodside and Seacombe: the two 9-foot-wide gangways to the main deck and an upstairs gangway 6 feet wide to the promenade deck. The upper gangway was not used in the off-peak.

WALLASEY FERRIES, 1950

Ferries from Seacombe and New Brighton landed at the next two berths down-river along the stage from the Woodside berth, with only 5 feet between stem and stern when all three ferries were in. Against the Birkenhead steamers, Wallasey Ferries looked broad and massive with their extra 8 feet of beam, the wheelhouse and telegraph boxes on a bridge spanning the promenade deck and the timber awning carried on the steel-frame superstructure over the promenade deck abaft the bridge. The largest of these steamers was licensed to carry 2,233 passengers.

These steamers were similar in length and general arrangement to the Birkenhead steamers and, like them, had black hulls, white superstructure and dark-brown wooden deckhouses. The funnels were white with broad black bands top and bottom, and the master and mate on the bridge, in their navy blue uniforms and white-topped caps, blended into the composition of black and white. With their 'W.C.F.' flags flying from the mastheads in the blustery wind, these ferries invited us to leave the industrial and commercial world of Birkenhead and Liverpool and sail away down-river to the sandy shores and quiet, sylvan streets of Wallasey. There were more women and children, fewer cloth caps and headscarves and more pin-stripes and tweed, more white, open-necked shirts.

The gangways went down on the decks with a heavy clatter of wood on wood and a ring of heavy iron from under the turntable – even the gangways sounded different. On board we noticed more differences. Hefty wooden sliding doors with the borough coat of arms and 'WCF' in the frosted glass kept the draughts out of the aisles across the main deck saloons between the gangway gates, forming vestibules to the saloons. The central port and starboard seating areas on the walkway around the saloons were enclosed as side cabins with portholes and sliding doors. The engine room ventilators on top were columnar and the ships' names on the bows were in conventional capital letters.

Not only were Wallasey ferries generically different from Birkenhead ferries, but each pair of sister ships was also different. Wallasey Corporation had seven steamers and one motor launch in 1950. *J. Farley* and *Francis Storey*, dating from 1922, were the last of the old, narrow steamers, being only 40 feet wide, like the Woodside steamers, and the last to be fitted with a canvas awning on the aft promenade deck. They were named after former chairmen of the Ferries Committee.

Wallasey and *Marlowe*, of 1927, were the first of the 48-foot-wide steamers, the first with solid timber awnings on the aft promenade deck and the first with twin rudders and cruiser sterns (instead of counter sterns). They were the most commodious ferry steamers on the Mersey, with certificates to carry 2,233 passengers.

Perch Rock, of 1929, was a loner; the last of the tubby, bluff-bowed, double-twin-screw goods ferries, 144 feet by 50 feet, she was converted in 1947 to a primitive passenger ferry with buoyant wooden seats on her vast deck and a certificate for 1,600 passengers. She augmented the two regular steamers on the New Brighton service at busy holiday times from 1948 to 1953.

Royal Iris II of 1932 and *Royal Daffodil II* of 1934 had a third deck aft the bridge and more hefty, wooden, sliding doors just as a windbreak on the promenade deck under the bridge. The third deck gave passengers a view of the officers working the helm and telegraphs on the bridge, but it did not increase the passenger capacity, which was slightly less than *Wallasey* and *Marlowe* at 2,024 and 1,995 passengers respectively. *Royal Iris II* was renamed *St*

Hilary after the patron saint of Wallasey in 1950, when the third *Royal Iris* was on the stocks at Dumbarton.

St *Hilary*'s saloons were built of the finest Burma teak and the main saloon was fitted out in Tudor style, with oak beams and panelled walls, leather upholstered seats and a 6 feet by 4 feet painting of the old *Iris* and *Daffodil* in the Zeebrugge raid in 1917. *Royal Daffodil II* was fitted out identically in 1934 but, after being bombed and sunk at Seacombe in 1941, was refitted in 1943 with austerity steel saloons. After the war she doubled as the cruise ship and was repainted with yellow hull and saloons and a buff funnel.

The odd one out in the history and evolution of the Mersey ferries was the wooden motor-launch TSMV *Wallasey Belle*, a 1944 ex-Royal Navy 'Fairmile' Class rescue launch that had been converted for short sea cruises at Bournemouth. Wallasey bought her in 1949 for Seacombe night service and river cruises, serving soup and tea in the cabin below deck. She was just a green hull, two buff funnels with green garters and an open cockpit on deck. She seemed very small to us, at 108 feet by 18 feet and 126 gross tons, but she was, in fact, larger than the pioneer paddle-steamers that had plied to Birkenhead and Wallasey in the 1820s, '30s and '40s. She proved to be strictly a fair-weather vessel and, with no shelter on deck, we could appreciate the hardiness of those early ferry passengers sailing on *Sir John Moore* to New Brighton. *Wallasey Belle* was withdrawn after an aggregate of less than 12 months' service, mainly in 1950, but she made history by being the first diesel ferry on the Mersey.

While all Birkenhead ferries were Birkenhead-built, Wallasey favoured Scottish shipbuilders, three of the Wallasey fleet in 1950 coming from Dundee, two from Troon and one from Govan. Only *Royal Daffodil II* was from the Tranmere yard. While Birkenhead ferries stuck to coal, four Wallasey steamers, *J. Farley*, *Wallasey*, *Marlowe* and *Royal Daffodil II*, were converted to oil-burners in 1946-47, and Wallasey began building diesel ferries 10 years before Birkenhead.

Wallasey ferries left Liverpool diagonally down-river. On the incoming tide the New Brighton ferry passed alongside the Irish Sea ferries and ocean liners berthed at Prince's Landing Stage,

and at high water, on its way down to the pier at the mouth of the river, it passed inbound and outbound ships that appeared and disappeared over the grey horizon. Seacombe Ferry headed for the 90-foot-tall Art Deco clock tower at the south end of Wallasey riverfront and the 480-foot-long landing stage with its long neo-Tudor timber-framed waiting shed, creaking on the tideway, springing from the rock-faced red sandstone river wall. Wallasey ferries carried no fenders, relying on the rubber tyres along the stage.

The steamer landed with all the ease and deft use of screws, current and ropes we had seen at Woodside. The swivelling gangway fell with its characteristic ring and again we were dosed with the salt, soot and sewage aromatherapy of the Mersey as we tramped across the drawbridge. We herded along the stage and bent our backs up the incline of the wide south bridge built in 1880 for the use of goods ferry traffic at high water in the days of the hydraulic lifts. At the top of the incline we entered the spacious Art Deco arrival booking-hall, echoing to whistling workmen in the crowd and clicking turnstiles. Outside, beyond the classical stone colonnade of the tollhouse, the yellow Wallasey buses made guttural sounds as they rumbled over the granite setts of Victoria Place bus station to await the passengers from the ferry.

As a boy, before submitting my 2d toll at the turnstiles, I always paused to pay my respects to the range of model ferry steamers in glass cases that in those days were displayed in the arrival hall. The models of specific steamers, with their details on plaques, showed the evolution of the ferry steamers from *Sir John Moore* of 1826 to *Royal Daffodil II* of 1934. The *Royal Iris* (1951) was added later. These models were later moved to the departure hall and are now in the Earlston Library in Upper Brighton. A similar collection of even finer models of Birkenhead ferries is on display in the Williamson Art Gallery & Museum, Birkenhead.

I lived in Wallasey from 1949 to 1952 and often returned home across the Mersey to Seacombe by night. The marine steam engines gave passengers a smooth, quiet ride; they could not be heard beyond the engine room and the ferries slipped across the river with no sound but their wash. On a calm night it was a wonderful experience to stand at the front of the promenade deck, heading into the inky blackness and fresh, salty air, as the steamer stole smoothly and silently across the river with just the sound of wavelets lapping the bow and the hiss of foam streaking along the sides, all sound of the screw wash being masked by the bulk of the ship and carried away in our slipstream. The tall, black-and-white funnel and the captain in his wheelhouse presided over us, the lonely masthead lantern was high aloft among the stars, and all was well in my world. This was bliss.

The Mersey was not always as calm as this, of course. The wind often dropped at dusk and got up at dawn. Some days it got up rough. I used to enjoy a stormy day on Seacombe Ferry, the more exposed of the two winter services, being nearer the river mouth. When a strong wind blew in from the Irish Sea during the school holidays, I took a box of sandwiches, bought a half-crown (2s 6d) all-day (child) ticket at Seacombe tollhouse and rode the ferry to Liverpool and back all day long. The landing stages creaked and squeaked as they heaved on the swell. On such days we could see why the steamers were so robustly built, and why *Wallasey Belle* was so ineffective. The big steamer

biffed into the landing stage once or twice before it was able to tie up. The whole stage shuddered and the big rubber tyre fenders screeched as they were contorted. The steamer wrenched at its mooring ropes as the passengers boarded by running at intervals over a narrow storm gangway that was not fixed to the stage but free to rise and fall with the varying levels between the decks of the stage and the steamer, which could be as much as 4 or 5 feet, when the gangway would be pitched at a steep angle. In such conditions the balanced gangways on turntables could have been damaged.

The broad-beamed steamer rolled heavily as it pitched its way across the raging river. While most passengers huddled in the saloon, I spent the whole day up on the promenade deck, seated or promenading, revelling in the wildness of it all and wishing it would pitch and roll deeper and higher. The main deck and the landing stages were wet with spray and we could see waves breaking over the riverside promenade between Seacombe and New Brighton. After a stormy day on Seacombe ferry, the streets of Wallasey and the rooms of my home were rolling up and down for fully two days afterwards!

I thought of the Emetty, long-funnelled paddle-steamers of the 1830s tossing about on Turneresque seas and landing at the primitive wooden piers and stone slipways, and the wooden run-out stages being derailed by the waves. I was regaled with tales of the New Ferry stage being carried away up-river, Woodside stage partly sinking in a storm in 1887, and New Brighton landing stage floating out to sea in a gale in 1907 – what a strange sight that must have been to incoming ships. In our own time Seacombe floating road was partly sunk in a storm in 1955, and the south bridge at New Brighton Pier was lifted off the stage by huge waves and sunk in 1962.

Another pleasure I had on the ferries was collecting the captain's autographs. It was not uncommon in those days for people to carry a pocket autograph book; every schoolboy carried a lot of things in his jacket pockets in those days, as every Richmal Crompton reader knows. I set out two double pages under the headings of 'Birkenhead Corporation Ferries' and 'Wallasey Corporation Ferries', and collected the autographs of all the captains in 1950-51, when I was aged 12-13. I would ask a deckhand for the captain's autograph – he never took the book but always took me in person to see the captain, who would usually be up on the bridge, but sometimes in his cabin down in the engine room, and was always obliging. Each steamer had three captains to cover the three 8-hour watches and one relief captain to cover sickness and holidays. This took me up to the bridge and down to the engine room on many a trip across the Mersey, which was every boy's wish

FROM STEAM TO DIESEL

My Steam Age bliss was shattered by the arrival of three diesel ferries in the Wallasey fleet in 1951-52. The 1950s was a decade of slow transition from the old order to the new. In 1950 there were 11 steamers and one rarely seen motor launch on the Mersey ferries. By 1960 there were six diesels and four steamers. By 1964 the last steamer had gone, leaving only seven diesels.

The first of the new generation, in 1951, was the diesel-electric Royal Iris, a dual-purpose cruise ship and ferry, a hideously futuristic but imaginatively streamlined version of the former cruise ship Royal

Daffodil II. She looked as if she had been designed by Frank Hampson, creator of Dan Dare in the Eagle boys' comic launched in 1950, but this was the style of the brave new post-war world set by the Austin Atlantic and Morris Minor motor cars of 1949 and the 1951 Festival of Britain. Royal Iris featured a 60 feet by 40 feet dance hall, a buffet, bar, tea room, ladies' rest room and a fish and chip saloon for cruising. She was known locally as the 'booze boat' (to rhyme with cruise boat), the 'fish and chip boat' or just the 'chip boat'. I called her the 'Royal Eyesore' because I thought she looked fat and ugly and quite un-nautical, especially from the bow view, although the custard-yellow superstructure and pale-green hull did not help her appearance. In her 1972 refit she became respectable, losing her chip shop, gaining a plush restaurant and being repainted white and blue.

She was popular for her internal appointments, and at least she continued the Wallasey tradition of 150 feet by 48 feet commodious Scottish-built ferries with massive timberwork in her decking and sliding doors, a ferrying licence for 2,296 passengers and a sea-cruising licence for 1,000. However, her gross tonnage, at 1,234, was twice that of her predecessors, being a measure of enclosed space (100 cubic feet to the ton), as she was totally enclosed except for a 'sun deck' on top, the equivalent of the third deck on Royal Daffodil II.

The next two diesel ferries, Leasowe of 1951 and Egremont of 1952, were of conventional, post-war motorship design, but broke with Wallasey tradition in being built at Dartmouth, and being only three-quarters of the size of their predecessors, 18 feet shorter and 14 feet narrower. They had only one gangway gate each side, aft, which slowed loading, and no sliding doors to the aisle between the saloons and the aft offices. With full-width saloons forward of the gate aisle, the only walkway round the main deck was at the stern. A semi-circular shelter on the forward promenade deck, together with the seating on a deck 14 feet narrower, restricted the path of the promenaders.

With no walkway around the fore end of the main deck, the deckhands on Leasowe and Egremont had no access to the bow ropes and bollards except by a small private door in the crowded saloon, or, in practice, by walking outside the bulwarks along the unusually wide rubbing strake, which seemed to have been provided to remedy this shortcoming. The four Mersey ferries that followed, in 1958-62, were larger and reverted to two transverse aisles between four gangway gates and a continuous walkway around the main deck.

Wallasey Corporation's last ship, *Royal Daffodil II* of 1958, was a bit of a throwback, being the last of the broad-beamed three-decker heavyweights from Scottish shipyards. She had the same dimensions and passenger capacity as her former steam namesake, now renamed *St Hilary*. She had teak rails not only around the main deck but also around the upper decks, where the steamers just had iron rails. There was, however, no reversion to sliding doors to the aisles between the saloons. More saloon accommodation on the second deck forced promenaders up to the third deck. I disliked the excess of solid white steel superstructure and the stepped windows of the forward saloons. She lacked the grace of the two remaining Wallasey steamers.

Birkenhead Corporation preferred to soldier on with its reliable steamers through the 1950s, then eclipsed them with three diesels in 1960-62. *Mountwood* and *Woodchurch* were built at Dartmouth in 1960 and *Overchurch* was built at Tranmere in 1962. They were a standard 142 feet by 39 feet and 464 tons, with passenger capacities of 1,200, all slightly less than their steam predecessors, which were also all standard, unlike Wallasey ferries.

In contrast to the handsomely proportioned, stealthy steamers with tall funnels and dark-brown deckhouses, the post-war diesel ferries were generally small, squat, noisy vessels with stumpy funnels and white, steel deckhouses. They looked smart from the side but ungainly from the front, with the foredeck shelter and the cliff-like bridge masking the funnel. Noisy diesel engines vibrated through the ship and could be heard from the far side of the river. The fumes were disgusting. They were, however, faster, cheaper to run and cleaner

to work than the old steamers, and some of them provided a bar and buffet for cruising.

Birkenhead's last steamer, *Claughton* of 1930, retired in 1961. Although Wallasey had begun to dieselise 10 years before Birkenhead, the transition was slower and the last steam ferry on the Mersey was *Wallasey* of 1927, which remained in service till 1963. Her departure for the breakers marked the end of 148 years of steam ferries on the river.

Cork harbour became a kind of Valhalla for the old Mersey steam ferries to live out second lives, unaltered but renamed, doubling as excursion steamers and tenders to trans-Atlantic liners. From 1927 to 1961 you could always find at least two ex-Mersey ferry steamers at Cork. There were the five ex-Wallasey ferries, *Rose* and *Lily* (1900-27), *Royal Iris* (1906-31), *John Joyce* (1910-36) and *Francis Storey* (1922-51), and the ex-Birkenhead ferry *Bidston* (1933-60). *Royal Iris*, of Zeebrugge fame, escorted them all in turn. She plied on Dublin Bay excursions from 1932 to 1938, and returned to Cork to rejoin *Rose* and *Lily* till they were scrapped in 1939, *John Joyce* till 1951, *Francis Storey* till 1959 and *Bidston* from 1960. *Royal Iris* had a major refit in 1946 and was reboiled in 1952; she was 55 years old and still fit to steam when she went to the breakers in 1961. *Bidston* followed her in 1962.

If ever a ship should have been brought back to the Mersey for preservation it was the original *Royal Iris*, but Philistines prevailed in the 1960s and we were throwing out everything old. A maritime museum had not even been conceived.

Mountwood, *Woodchurch* and *Overchurch* were the last ferries bought by Birkenhead Corporation before the amalgamation of the Mersey ferries in 1969, and, with the demise of the Wallasey fleet, these three ex-Birkenhead vessels alone carry on the much modified Mersey ferry service and cruises today. Refitted and renamed, they hark back to Birkenhead's red and black funnels and carry traditional Wallasey ferry names, respectively *Royal Iris*, *Snowdrop* and *Royal Daffodil*.

Right An advertisement for Birkenhead Corporation Ferries from the 1951 Birkenhead Official Guide, showing the twin-screw steamer *Hinderton* (1925-58).

Below The wooden **WOODSIDE FERRY TOLLHOUSE**, with its iron colonnade and clock in the dormer gable, was built in 1864. The great shed housed the tollbooths, turnstiles and offices of Birkenhead Corporation Ferries, together with the Corporation bus inspectors', inquiries and lost property offices, William Clayton's barber shop, Finlay's tobacconist kiosk, Mrs Mary Thorburn's refreshment room, W. H. Smith's newspaper stall and Noblett's confectionery stall. An extension in front of the bus inspectors' office, at the left-hand end of the colonnade, housed the Avoca Tea Rooms, busy with bus crews. The ferry entrance was built on the river wall on reclaimed land jutting out from the natural river bank at the foot of the slope below the Woodside Hotel.

This humble shed, seen here in 1976, was the focal point of life in Birkenhead. All roads led ultimately to Woodside Ferry, and it was the existence of this ferry passage across the Mersey to Liverpool and the advent of steam ferries here in 1822 that led to the growth of Birkenhead, and the lifeblood of the town flowed through the ferry terminus in daily communion with Liverpool. The pioneer British horse tramway of the Birkenhead Street Railway Company in 1860 ran from the Woodside Hotel to Birkenhead Park and was extended to Oxton in 1861, and to this ferry entrance when the new ferry approach and terminus were completed in 1864. In 1878 the Birkenhead Joint Railway of the LNWR and GWR was extended to a new terminus on the right hand side of the ferry approach. Birkenhead Corporation laid a six-track electric tram terminus in this forecourt in 1901, and from 1925 and 1930 respectively, Birkenhead and Crosville buses came to Woodside Ferry and turned round here, unloading passengers at the

BIRKENHEAD
CORPORATION
FERRIES

Provide an interesting, healthy and speedy service between Birkenhead and Liverpool

REGULAR DAY and NIGHT SERVICE

★

River Cruises for Private Parties by Arrangement

★

An excellent way of seeing the River Front and Shipping on the River

★

Through Ferry and Bus tickets are issued at cheap rates to all parts of Birkenhead and to many interesting places in Wirral

colonnade before moving on to their loading berths outside the railway station. The paint scheme of the ferry buildings was green and cream and the painted lettering 'FERRY TO LIVERPOOL' was emblazoned along the roof.

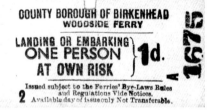

Top Passengers to and from Liverpool paid at the **WOODSIDE FERRY TOLLBOOTHS** inside the booking hall and passed through the turnstiles. Tolls were 2½d for adults and 1d for children (aged three to 14) from 1948 till 1955. The peak year on the Woodside Ferry was 1926-27 when 14,093,135 passengers passed through the turnstiles. The post-war peak was 11,400,795 passengers in 1948-49. The 1950s saw a steady decline from 11,098,928 passengers in 1949-50 to 6,985,000 in 1959-60. Paintwork in the booking hall was green and cream.

Left After passing through the booking hall on the river wall, passengers walked down the **BRIDGE TO THE LANDING STAGE**. The bridge was hinged to the river wall and the floating stage to allow for the 31-foot tidal range in the Mersey estuary. At high water the bridge was level, but at low water it was quite steep to walk up and down. Dating from 1862, the bridge had twin walkways to divide the flows of passengers to and from Liverpool, and in 1863 was covered by a twin, barrel-vaulted glazed roof, reglazed in 1904. This 1976 view shows passengers embarking for Liverpool; those landing at Woodside walked up the twin adjoining walkway on the left. The twin barrels sprang from the columns on the left-hand side of this arcade and the wooden partition divided them from the disembarking passengers till they reached the turnstiles.

Above Viewed here from an approaching ferry, the **WOODSIDE FERRY LANDING STAGE** was 800 feet long and 80 feet wide. The south end, pictured here in 1978 with its barrel-vaulted waiting shed, was used by passenger ferries. The middle section was used by goods (vehicular) ferries from 1868 to 1941, and for coaling ferries and tugs, while the north end was used for landing cattle, sheep and pigs at the adjacent lairage from 1878 till 1981. The stage was joined to the river wall by two hinged bridges, one for passengers and the other for cattle, by the hinged sections of the floating road on pontoons to the goods ferry and by a hinged boom. The picture shows the covered passenger bridge from the river wall (left), the open promenade deck for waiting passengers on the south end with access from the waiting room door, the top deck gangway used at peak times, the two main deck gangways and the marker light and fog bell tower (extreme right). Behind the stage we can see the roofs of the Woodside lairage and part of the Woodside ventilation shaft (extreme right) of the road tunnel that eclipsed the vehicular ferry.

Woodside Stage was built on the West Float, secured to the river wall here in 1861, and commissioned in 1862. The waiting shed and the roof over the passenger bridge were added in 1863. The stage was 123 years old and thought to be the oldest floating structure in the world when it was towed away for demolition in Liverpool docks in 1985, to be replaced with a short, one-berth stage that retains some of the hardware from the old stage and echoes the barrel-vaulted bridge and waiting shed.

Right Two drawbridge gangways on turntables dropped with a loud clack of wood on wood on to the timber deck of the ferry steamer and a jingle of chains. A strong whiff of salt water assailed the nostrils as passengers trooped across the gap between stage and steamer. This photograph shows the spiral pattern on the iron columns supporting the barrel-vaulted

wooden roof on the landing stage. The stage was moored to the river wall by surplus stock of huge chains made for Brunel's 1863 steamship *Great Eastern* by Henry Wood's chain and anchor foundry at Saltney near Chester. Turn-round time at the landing stage was a hectic 3 minutes in peak periods and a leisurely 8 minutes in the off-peak before departure.

Above   Nine pontoons comprised the 677-foot-long **WOODSIDE FERRY FLOATING ROAD** down to the goods ferry. It had steel-plate runways for vehicles, with central wood-block paths for draught horses and boardwalks on each side, making a total width of 30 feet. It opened in 1868, when goods, hand-carts and horse-drawn vehicles were shipped across the river by converted passenger steamer. A fleet of purpose-built, double-twin-screw, flush-decked goods ferries operated from the middle section of Woodside Stage to the foot of the floating road on Liverpool Stage from 1879 till the closure of the service in 1941, seven years after the opening of the Mersey road tunnel.

At low water the gradient of the floating road was too steep for horse-drawn vehicles, and at high water the road undulated as the waves rolled in. After the closure of the goods ferry the road was still used by cyclists using the passenger ferry and by lorries delivering coal bags to the stage for ferry steamers and tugs at the old goods ferry berth; indeed, so many cyclists used the ferry that they had their own toll collector on the stage.

On the right is the Birkenhead Corporation bus storage road on the site of the 1823 stone slipway and the 1835 stone pier, and on the left are the cattle sheds of the Woodside lairage, where cattle, sheep and pigs were landed on the north end of Woodside

Stage. In the stone wall beneath the lairage were arches from which gushed water pumped out of the Mersey Railway tunnel by Shore Road Pumping Station. In 1954 two little girls stand on the left-hand boardwalk, and there is a group of cyclists at the end of the floating road, one of whom is pedalling up the right-hand boardwalk. In the background, just over half a mile across the Mersey, are the warehouses that formed a quadrangle around Albert Dock, Liverpool (1845). The Woodside floating road was closed in 1955 and removed in 1958.

Left From the foot of the floating road we see the twin-screw ferry steamer *Bidston* arriving at **WOODSIDE LANDING STAGE** from Liverpool in 1954. On the right are the barrel-roofed bridge and wooden waiting shed, the light and fog bell tower and – a mile and a half away across the river – the bulk of Liverpool Cathedral on the city skyline.

Above This 1954 stern view shows the 41-foot beam of the Birkenhead ferry steamer *Bidston* berthed at Woodside Landing Stage and the silhouette of the captain in the starboard-side telegraph box. The *Bidston* was built by Cammell, Laird at Tranmere in 1933, the youngest of the Birkenhead Corporation fleet of four steamers in the 1950s. It was 150 feet long, 487 gross tons, and licensed to carry 1,433 passengers. Also visible are the iron mooring chains, bollards and chain fence of the 1861-62 stage, one of the ornate lamp posts, the silhouette of the fog bell in the light tower, the gangway posts and the gangways in the raised position. The ferry passage to Liverpool was three-quarters of a mile. On the extreme left of the picture Dingle Point can be glimpsed on the Lancashire bank, where the river is a mile and a quarter wide. The visitor arriving at Birkenhead might think this view was looking out to sea, but we are in fact looking up-river, where the Mersey widens to 3 miles in its upper estuary between Ellesmere Port, Cheshire, and Oglet, Lancashire.

The steamer *Bidston* was in service on the Woodside Ferry from 1933 till 1960. Her superstructure was damaged by flying debris while berthed at Liverpool Landing Stage in the 1941 blitz. In 1960 Birkenhead chartered the vessel to the Harbour Commissioners at Cork, where it escorted and succeeded the famed ex-Wallasey ferry *Royal Iris* of 1906 as a tender to trans-Atlantic liners and an excursion steamer. It was sold in 1962 to Cork shipbreakers and broken up nearby at Ballinacurra.

Below A painting of Woodside Ferry in 1814 by William G. Herdman. *Williamson Art Gallery, Birkenhead*

Above The Birkenhead steamer **HINDERTON**, seen here in 1950 approaching Woodside, dated back to 1925 and set the standard design for the Corporation ferry fleet until 1960. She was the first Birkenhead ferry with full-width promenade decks, giving shelter to the walkway around the saloons on the main deck. She was also the prototype for her three consorts, which followed in 1930-33 to provide the Liverpool-Woodside ferry service through the 1930s, '40s and '50s. They were all twin-screw steamers built by Cammell, Laird at Tranmere, each 150 feet long, 41 feet in the beam, licensed to carry 1,433 passengers, and all coal-fired to the end. *Hinderton*, at 484 gross tons, was 3 tons less than *Thurstaston, Claughton* or *Bidston*. Birkenhead Corporation always gave its ferries local place names, *Hinderton* being the old name of Lower Tranmere, where she was built. The last Rock Ferry steamer, *Upton*, which

followed *Hinderton* off the slips at Tranmere in 1925, was a similar design but smaller at 145 feet by 32 feet and 462 tons.

Birkenhead used *Hinderton* for summer excursions from Woodside and Liverpool down-river to the Bar lightship and up-river off Eastham, with a canvas awning rigged up over the promenade deck on the temporary framework we can see aft of the funnel. These trips were run occasionally in the war years 1942-44 and regularly from 1945 to 1948. In the early 1950s *Hinderton* was occasionally seen on charter to Wallasey Corporation as a relief ferry on the Seacombe and New Brighton services. *Hinderton* retired from service in 1956 after two mid-river collisions made her hull plates unsafe. She was laid up in dock till 1958, when she was sold to Dutch breakers and towed to Antwerp for scrap.

In this picture, taken from Woodside Stage, we can also see, through the smoky haze, the massive granaries at Coburg Dock, Liverpool: a brick silo of 1906 (left) and a concrete one of 1936, linked by a high-level covered footbridge.

Left Looming out of the smoky gloom on the Mersey as it drifts in to Woodside Landing Stage against the incoming tide, also in 1950, **THURSTASTON** (150 feet, 487 gross tons) was built in 1930 and plied the Liverpool-Woodside ferry service for 31 years. Birkenhead Corporation ferries of this period were distinguished from Wallasey ferries by having the wheelhouse and side telegraph boxes on deck instead of on a bridge, by their names in cursive, italic script on the bow, and by the rope fenders hanging along the rubbing strake. Funnels were Indian red and black, while the hulls were black above the white waterline with a red stripe above the rubbing strake, and red below the waterline. The superstructure was white, and the navigation boxes were dark brown varnished wood. The temporary framework for a canvas awning can be seen aft of the funnel, but the canvas was so rarely used on Birkenhead ferries that the framework was later removed. *Thurstaston* was sold in 1961 to a Dutch trading company and is thought to have been broken up in 1965.

Above The last Birkenhead steam ferry on the Mersey was **CLAUGHTON** (150 feet, 487 gross tons), built in 1930. Like her elder sisters *Hinderton* and *Thurstaston*, she plied the Woodside service for 31 years, soldiering on six months after the departure of the latter. On passage from Woodside to Liverpool, she is ploughing through choppy water in mid-river, fringed with surf, bristling with rope fenders, a wisp of steam from her whistle on the funnel as she salutes the ferry passing in the opposite direction, from which this photograph was taken in 1961. The summer evening sunlight casts shadows from the waves on the water and picks out the light Indian red and black paint scheme on the funnel: there was a broad black band top and bottom with a black hoop halfway.

The sun also lights up the pale green hull of the Shell tanker *Sepia* (42,000 gross tons) in the fitting-out basin at Cammell, Laird's shipyard on Tranmere shore in the background, where *Claughton* and her three sister steamers were built. The yards covered 1,033 yards of riverfront and 108 acres of reclaimed land, and employed more than 10,000 men when they were busy. *Claughton* retired from service at the end of 1961 and was towed away in company with Wallasey's *St Hilary* (ex-*Royal Daffodil II*) to a Belgian breakers' yard in 1962. The new tanker *Sepia* was in service till 1983. Oil tankers were taking over from colliers on the Mersey, and in the distance over the bow of the ferry steamer, we can see Tranmere Oil Terminal, which opened in 1960. Oil was piped to storage tanks on the shore, then to Stanlow refinery.

Below Passengers were not allowed to smoke on the **WOODSIDE FERRY**, even on the open promenade deck, although it was usually too windy for anyone to light up. There was, however, smoke from the funnel and, as we turn away from Woodside for Liverpool, over the bow we can see the three smoking chimneys of Clarence Dock Power Station of the Merseyside & North Wales Electricity Board. The Royal Liver Building is on the extreme right. Another distinguishing feature of a Birkenhead ferry steamer were the two Punch & Judy-style cabinets abaft the funnel, which were engine room ventilator cowls. Although the pulsation of the steam engines could not be heard or felt by passengers in the saloons, the sounds of the engine room and its telegraph bell could be heard from these cowls and from the engine room companionways on the main deck. The cowls were varnished dark brown like the wheelhouse forward of the funnel and the port and starboard telegraph boxes; their steel inner lining was painted light ochre red to match the funnel. Among those taking the air on the top deck in 1954 are a white-collar worker in a trilby hat and mackintosh and a labourer in cloth cap and overalls.

Above Liverpool-bound passengers enjoy the fresh, salty air and close-up views of shipping on the Mersey from the relative shelter of the starboard walkway on the main deck of a Birkenhead ferry steamer crossing the river from Woodside. The three-quarter-mile crossing took 7 minutes, and two steamers plied the service, passing in mid-river. This photograph, from the semi-enclosed seating area on the walkway, shows the stairs with their brass handrails to the forward promenade deck and the huge, python-like ropes draped over the bulwarks next to the gangway gate. Liverpool waterfront lies ahead on the starboard bow, and we can glimpse a black and white Wallasey ferry leaving the landing stage, the soot-black Royal Liver Building, and the steeple of St Nicholas Parish Church with its lantern tower.

Below Two Birkenhead ferries pass in mid-river at a combined speed of 28 knots; we are bound for Liverpool and, seen from the aisle across the deck between the gangway gates, the other ferry is on its way back to Woodside. Two smart sports cycles lean against the massive, varnished woodwork of the forward saloon (Woodside Ferry was a popular route for cyclists between Liverpool and North Wales), a brass handrail leads upstairs to the promenade deck, and mooring ropes casually festoon the bulwarks. In the background are the five-storey Albert Dock warehouses of 1845 and the tower of Liverpool Cathedral.

The Birkenhead Corporation ferry steamer *Bidston* (1933) cuts an anachronistic figure with its tall funnel and rope fenders as it edges into its berth at the south end of **GEORGE'S LANDING STAGE, LIVERPOOL**, in 1958, nicely framed between the stage furniture. On the right we see the New Brighton Ferry berth with the stairs to the top deck gangway and the gangway posts to the main deck. Beyond the line of crush barriers for rush-hours and bank holidays we see the Seacombe Ferry berth with its upper and lower gangways and the slotted-post semaphore destination sign. Beyond the fog bell tower is the Woodside Ferry berth, where *Bidston* will tie up. *Liverpool Daily Post, by courtesy of Trinity Mirror North West & North Wales Ltd*

Left At the Woodside berth on **GEORGE'S LANDING STAGE**, passengers passed under an ornate Victorian arch with lacy spandrels and pediment, the words 'WOODSIDE FERRY' stencilled in a rope-framed panel on the lintel, all in cast-iron, and pendant gas lamps – a design straight out of the pages of Rowland Emett. Two arches like this spanned the two swivelling gangways on to the deck of the Birkenhead ferry to Woodside, this one forward, the other aft, dating from the opening of the landing stage in 1876. Originally these ornate arches were hung with globular lamps in place of the pendant lamps we see here. Small crown finials on the gangway posts symbolised King Edward III's charter of 1330 granting the monks of Birkenhead Priory and their 'successors for ever' the right of passage across the 'arm of the sea' and to charge tolls. Extant records show that the ferry was already in existence in 1282.

In this 1954 view the poster board is advertising a nightly dancing programme at New Brighton Tower Ballroom, and Liverpool's own song and dance entertainer, Frankie Vaughan, is due to appear at the Tower Theatre. In 1957 he starred as a Teddy Boy gang leader in the film *These Dangerous Years*, partly set on Liverpool waterfront. The film opened with a scene on Woodside Ferry.

Below Returning across the river in 1954, the **BIRKENHEAD FERRY** swings out from Liverpool Landing Stage into the flood tide and Wallasey's dockside mills hove into view over the port bulwark as we turn towards Woodside. A deckhand leans over the rail beside the mooring ropes, and a small boy, leaning against the gangway gate, is wearing the customary school cap

and blazer in the school holidays. Passengers sample the healthy route between Liverpool and Birkenhead and the brass handrail beckons us upstairs to the promenade deck for a wider view of the riverfront and shipping.

Above This stirring view shows the promenade deck of a Birkenhead ferry with the captain and mate in the wheelhouse as we leave Liverpool's dramatic waterfront and head for Woodside. The dignified waterfront offices were built on the site of the filled-in George's Dock between 1903 and 1916; from right to left, they are the Dock Office, the Cunard Building and the Royal Liver Building. They formed the theatrical backdrop to George's Landing Stage and the tram terminus on George's

Pier Head. A black and white Wallasey ferry steamer astern ignores the 'No Smoking' order as its swings out from the stage towards Seacombe! *Commercial postcard*

Below The abiding impression of Merseyside in the 1950s and before was one of ships, cranes and smoke-stacks, but if there was one image, like Tower Bridge and the Pool of London, that represented Merseyside more than any other, it was this picture of the soot-stained buildings on Liverpool Pier Head lording over the Mersey scene, and a ferry steaming across the river. The Birkenhead Corporation ferry steamer *Bidston* (1933-60) ploughs its foamy furrow across the river on its return trip to Woodside. *Commercial postcard*

Above **MOUNTWOOD**, Birkenhead's first diesel ferry, approaches Liverpool Landing Stage in 1964, a storm light glinting on the Mersey under a grim cloud over Birkenhead and the shipyards. *Mountwood* was built in 1959 by Philip & Son at Dartmouth with Crossley diesel engines, and entered service in 1960. She was the prototype of the new generation of Birkenhead diesel ferries, slightly smaller than the steamers at 142 feet by 39 feet with a 1,200-passenger capacity, and the first Birkenhead ferries with a bridge spanning the promenade deck. Thanks to a major refit in dry dock in 1990 (when a fully covered bridge altered her appearance), *Mountwood* has been in Mersey ferry service now for more than 45 years – longer than any other vessel – and is still with us today, renamed *Royal Iris*.

Below Her twin screws churning the water and the captain silhouetted in the starboard-side telegraph box, **WOODCHURCH** swings out from Liverpool Landing Stage on a flood tide and heads for Woodside. This stern view from 1964 shows her short funnel, which is masked by the bridge when looking from the bow. She wears the Birkenhead Corporation funnel colours of light Indian red with a black top and a black hoop. *Woodchurch* was the sister ship of *Mountwood* with the same statistics, following her sister off the stocks at Dartmouth in 1959 and into service in 1960. She was laid up for sale in Morpeth Dock from 1981 to 1983, but was then overhauled for further ferry service. Following a major refit in 1989 (also with a fully covered bridge) she and her sister *Mountwood* are still plying between Woodside and Liverpool today – and now also from Seacombe, following the amalgamation of the Mersey ferries in 1969 and the demise of the Wallasey fleet. She is now named *Snowdrop*.

Far right An advertisement for Wallasey Corporation Ferries from the 1950 City of Liverpool Official Handbook, showing the twin-screw steamer *Royal Daffodil II* (1934-58).

Below A blustery west wind whips the smoke from the funnels, choppy water slaps the hulls, and gulls wheel around the Wallasey Corporation ferries *Royal Daffodil II* and *Marlowe*, with their 'W.C.F'. red flags flying from the mastheads, at the Seacombe and New Brighton berths of **GEORGE'S LANDING STAGE, LIVERPOOL**. Wallasey Ferries favoured Scottish shipyards, and *Royal Daffodil II* (nearer the camera) was one of only four vessels built for Wallasey Ferries (company and municipal) at Tranmere in a line of 69 vessels from the first steamship in 1822 to the last motorship in 1958. She was built in 1934 to replace the famous *Royal Daffodil* (1906-33), which earned its Royal prefix for its part in the First World War blockade of Zeebrugge. She was 151 feet long, 46 feet in the beam, 580 gross tons and, although a three-decker, was licensed to carry only 1,995 passengers compared with the 2,233 passenger capacity of the two-decker *Marlowe* astern. Her beautiful teak and oak saloons were replaced with utility steel saloons in a 1942-43 refit after being sunk by a bomb at Seacombe stage in the 1941 blitz.

To celebrate the end of the war in 1945 *Royal Daffodil II* embarked on dance cruises from Liverpool and New Brighton, which were so popular with post-war holidaymakers from the Midlands and the North that she doubled as a regular cruise ship, with yellow hull and buff funnel, till 1950. When the new cruise ship, the TSMV *Royal Iris* arrived in 1951, *Royal Daffodil II* reverted to full-time ferry service in black and white. She was renamed *St Hilary* when the new motorship *Royal Daffodil II* arrived in 1958, and she continued in service till 1962, when she was towed away in company with Birkenhead's last steam ferry *Claughton* to a Belgian breaker's yard. On the landing stage we see the wooden tower housing the fog bell, erected in 1926 to replace the old fog bell tower, and the Woodside ferry berth (right). The view was taken from the stern of a Birkenhead ferry leaving for Woodside in 1952.

Wallasey Corporation Ferries

The Ferry Services Provided by the Corporation are Unique!

In addition to the REGULAR SERVICE to **SEACOMBE AND NEW BRIGHTON A SPECIALLY APPOINTED STEAMER** upon which **refreshments** may be obtained and a **Dance Orchestra** is provided, also **Licensed Bar**, will make **River & Short Sea Cruises** during the **Summer Season** thereby providing a pleasant means for enjoying the **Sea Breezes** and seeing Ocean Liners passing in and out of the port.

Large Modern Passenger Steamers sail from Liverpool to Wallasey every few minutes and provide a rapid, pleasant and inexpensive means of communication across the River Mersey.

Day and **Night** Service.   Cheap Day Return Tickets

Travel in the Sunshine and Fresh Air

For further information apply to : **Ferries General Manager,** SEACOMBE FERRY, WALLASEY   Telephone Wallasey 3671/2

Above The broad-beamed character of the Wallasey ferries is shown in this 1952 photograph of **MARLOWE** at the New Brighton berth on Liverpool Landing Stage, taken from the top deck of *Royal Daffodil II* arriving at the Seacombe berth. Wallasey ferries were distinguished from the Birkenhead vessels not only by their greater breadth but also by the navigation boxes on a bridge that spanned the promenade deck, the black and white funnels (with a black band at the base of the funnel as well), and by the steel superstructure and timber awning over the promenade deck abaft the bridge. They did not carry rope fenders but relied on the giant rubber tyres on the landing stages.

Marlowe was built in 1927 by the Caledon Shipbuilding & Engineering Company at Dundee and, with her sister ship *Wallasey*, set a new standard of size and design for Wallasey ferries, being 151 feet long, 48 feet in the beam, 606 gross tons, a cruiser stern and twin rudders, and licensed to carry 2,233 passengers. She served Seacombe, Egremont and New Brighton

for 31 years and was sold in 1958 to the British Iron & Steel Corporation for scrap. In the background is Liverpool Riverside railway station for liner passengers, and the three smoking chimneys of Clarence Dock Power Station. Riverside station (1895-1971) was owned by the Mersey Docks & Harbour Board and used by LNWR/LMS trains, which ran non-stop between Riverside and Euston, and by troop trains. The railway reached Riverside from Edge Hill over the Waterloo Dock goods branch through Waterloo Tunnel and Waterloo goods station and across the dock road and Prince's Dock swing-bridge.

Below Seen approaching Liverpool Landing Stage from Seacombe in 1954, the steamer **WALLASEY** was also built by Caledon at Dundee in 1927 to the same specifications as her sister ship *Marlowe*. These two steamers provided the staple year-round service to Seacombe for more than 30 years. The passenger capacity of 2,233 made them ideal for the businessmen's peak services to Seacombe or for the holiday traffic to New Brighton between business peaks in summer. In the 1950s *Wallasey* also worked cruises up the Ship Canal to Pomona Docks, Manchester. The ships were built as coal-burners and were converted to oil-burners in their post-war refits. All Mersey steam ferries were built with a single foremast, as seen in the photographs of *Hinderton*, *Thurstaston* and *Marlowe*, but from 1954 they were fitted with a taller mainmast aft, as seen here, to carry a second white navigation light required by law for ships 150 feet long or more. Sunlight scintillates on the wake of the ferry and the cranes of Tranmere shipyard can be glimpsed astern.

Right 'All aboard for New Brighton.' Children line the rail on the promenade deck of **WALLASEY**, a deckhand is ready to raise the gangway and close the rolling gate in the bulwark, and the captain is in the wheelhouse in his white-topped cap ready to leave Liverpool Landing Stage for the 3-mile, half-hour passage down-river to New Brighton Pier on a sunny August day in 1956. New Brighton Ferry operated from Easter to October.

Below Ferries for Seacombe (right) and Woodside are berthed at **GEORGE'S LANDING STAGE, LIVERPOOL**, in 1954, and the fog bell tower is silhouetted between the gangway posts at the two berths. The landing stage is quiet now in the mid-morning lull. The broad deck was exposed to the weather between the ferry berths and the long waiting shed (left) at the back of the stage, but inside the shed were W. H. McConnell's Riverside Restaurant, a sweet kiosk and left luggage office, two news stands (Taylor's and Margaret Wythe's) and Finlay's tobacconist kiosk.

George's Landing Stage for Mersey ferries formed the south end of Liverpool Landing Stage, combining Prince's Stage with berths for Irish Sea ferries and ocean liners at the north end. The combined stage was 80 feet wide and 2,533 feet long, the largest floating structure in the world. It was built at Thomas Brassey's Canada Works on the West Float at Birkenhead in 1874, and rebuilt in 1876 after a fire. It was moored to the river wall from George's Dock pier to replace an earlier George's Stage of 1847, and came complete with a floating road for goods

ferry traffic. The first Prince's Stage was a separate stage moored off Prince's Dock in 1858 for the larger ships, but the second one, of 1896, was joined to the north end of George's Stage at the foot of the floating road, which now serviced the Irish Sea ferries and ocean liners, and George's Stage was extended south by 55 feet in 1922. George's Dock was filled in about 1900 to provide sites for the Liver, Cunard and Dock buildings, but the pier that enclosed the dock is still called George's Pier Head, or just Pier Head. After the last liner left Liverpool in 1972, the ferries berthed at Prince's Stage from 1973 to 1975, while this George's Stage was removed and replaced with a short, concrete floating stage for Mersey and Manx ferries, with a vehicular bridge. Prince's Stage and the floating road were then removed without replacement.

In this flashback view of GEORGE'S LANDING STAGE, LIVERPOOL, in 1925, the heyday of the goods ferries, we see horse-drawn, steam and petrol vehicles queuing at the foot of the floating road while others disembark from a Wallasey goods ferry steamer, and a fully loaded Birkenhead goods ferry arrives. Passenger ferries for New Brighton, Seacombe and Woodside are lined up along the stage in the background.

The goods ferry steamers were broad, bluff-bowed, single-ended vessels with twin-screws at each end for better manoeuvrability at the stages. The larger and heavier goods ferry gangways were mounted on board the steamers and powered from the steam engines.

With the extension of George's Stage in 1922, a second berth was provided for Birkenhead goods ferries to help shift the traffic. The increase in motor traffic after the First World War saw long queues of vehicles from the floating roads in the streets, and congestion on the stage, with the conflict between vehicles disembarking and those waiting to embark. The increasing congestion was only relieved by the opening of the Mersey Tunnel in 1934. The goods ferries continued to ply, mainly for horse-drawn traffic, to Woodside till 1941 and to Seacombe till 1947. *Liverpool Public Libraries, reproduced by permission of Liverpool Record Office*

Above The stern of *Wallasey*, loading for Seacombe, is viewed from the bow of a Birkenhead ferry at **GEORGE'S LANDING STAGE, LIVERPOOL**. The practised ferry crews deftly swung these tubby vessels into their berths and tied them fast to the stage with only 5 feet to spare between the bows and sterns of the Woodside, Seacombe and New Brighton steamers, sometimes in a 6-knot tide race or a westerly gale. The aft gangway bridges the gap between the stage and the main deck; the upper deck gangway, for peak-time loading only, is folded up in this off-peak scene in 1954, and there is another gangway to the main deck forward. The upstairs gangway is perched on top of the stagemen's hut. The large waiting shed (right) along the back of the landing stage included waiting rooms, the Riverside Restaurant, a left luggage office, a bookstall, a news stand, a tobacconist's kiosk and a sweet kiosk. The two high-level transverse breaks in the roof line are the arcaded entrances to two of the three covered passenger bridges that sloped up to the tram terminus on George's Pier Head. The bridges carried narrow cantilevered sidewalks outside the enclosed main walkways, used by the more intrepid passengers in a hurry.

Right The black and white funnel and starboard-side telegraph box tower above George's Landing Stage as passengers walk down the broad gangway on to the main deck of the ferry steamer for Seacombe. There was a second gangway to the main deck aft. Even the Wallasey ferry gangways made a different sound from the Birkenhead gangways, going down with a heavier clatter of wood on wood and a resonant, mellow ring of iron, like a big tramcar gong, from the turntables and gangway posts as they gently rocked. This 1954 view shows the wooden steps to the upper deck gangway to speed up loading in peak periods and, to the right, the slotted-post semaphore destination board showing 'SEACOMBE' (now in the author's collection). This rope-worked post with its circular top was a traditional feature on the promenade decks of the old Wallasey paddle-steamers, and was transferred to the landing stage.

Above There was more space to walk around the beamier **WALLASEY FERRY**. The broader side walkway around the main deck had an enclosed seating area on each side, walled in with portholes, and heavy wooden sliding doors helped to keep out the draughts. The monogram 'WCF' (Wallasey Corporation Ferries) can be seen etched in the glass of the door behind the pipe-smoker on the right of this 1954 photograph, and the Wallasey County Borough arms were frosted in the glass of the rolling doors to the vestibule of the main saloon (left). Tranmere shipyard cranes are glimpsed on the far shore over the rolling gate in the port-side bulwark. The notice on the deck above reads: 'Passengers are warned not to cross the brass line until the gangway plank is lowered.' The brass strip laid into the wooden deck marked the area where the gangway dropped on to the deck.

Left Passengers enjoy a grand view of Mersey shipping and the salty air of the estuary from the foredeck of the ferry steamer **WALLASEY** as she plies across the river from Liverpool to Seacombe in 1954. The tall black and white funnel lords over all, sporting its vertical brass, organ-pipe, trombone steam whistle and its horizontal foghorn. The dark-brown varnished bridge spans the deck. The mate is in the wheelhouse and the captain is on the bridge looking astern. The brass bell, engraved with the name of the ship, now hangs in Wallasey Town Hall.

Above right The Liverpool waterfront recedes astern as the ferry *Wallasey* steams towards Seacombe. This 1954 photograph provides details of the covered promenade deck aft of the bridge, which allowed for all-weather promenading except on the exposed foredeck. It was the custom of Wallasey businessmen travelling by ferry in the peak periods to pace around the promenade deck two or three abreast in a counter-clockwise direction, with their bowler hats and briefcases, trilby hats and mackintoshes, for the entire time they were on board between crossing the upper-deck gangways on each side of the river. The same ritual was observed by Birkenhead businessmen, but they had to do their promenading entirely alfresco. Most of the seats on the promenade deck were buoyant wooden seats with rope

and wood handles hanging on each side for use as life rafts in case the ferry sank before it reached Seacombe. This never happened, although there was a risk of collision during foggy or stormy passages across the shipping lanes.

Below Rising from the top deck of **ROYAL DAFFODIL II**, the columnar engine-room ventilator cowls were a feature of Wallasey ferries, and the wooden shelter over the central stairway to the lower deck was unique to this ship among the three-deckers. The sister ships *St Hilary* and *Royal Daffodil II* were the only three-deckers in the Mersey ferry fleets in 1950, but two later Wallasey diesel ferries, *Royal Iris* of 1951 and the new *Royal Daffodil II* of 1958, were also built as three-deckers. The wind whistles through the funnel's guy ropes as we ply the passage from Liverpool to Seacombe in 1952, and pass one of the small diesel ferries, *Leasowe* or *Egremont*, on its return trip. The grey outline of Wallasey and its Town Hall tower can be seen on the starboard bow.

Below Last of the old line of Wallasey's narrower ferry steamers were the sister ships *J. Farley* and *Francis Storey* of 1922, which saw 30 years' service into the early 1950s. They were similar in design and dimensions to the famous *Iris* and *Daffodil* of 1906, so this traditional Wallasey ferry design was seen on the Mersey for 46 years. The graceful proportions of these narrower steamers is shown in this portrait of **J. FARLEY** arriving at New Brighton on a cruise, with a canvas windbreak around her foredeck rail. The pair were built by Ailsa Shipbuilding & Engineering Company at Troon, Ayrshire, 152 feet long, 40 feet wide and 464 gross tons, licensed to carry 1,629 passengers.

John Farley and Francis Storey were the present and past chairmen of Wallasey Ferries Committee when the ships were named, and the pair worked the Seacombe Ferry till 1927, then transferred to Egremont and New Brighton. Both were requisitioned by the Admiralty during the Second World War, officered and manned by their ferry crews, augmented by RN officers and ratings, to fit torpedo nets to merchant ships in the Western Approaches; *J. Farley* was commissioned in 1943 to work in Milford Haven and the Firth of Clyde. After the war they were reconditioned, *J. Farley* being converted to an oil-burner and returning to ferry service in 1946. She was sometimes deployed on part-time cruise duty in the post-war period with trips up the Ship Canal to Manchester. The open promenade deck abaft her bridge was covered in 1948 with a timber awning on a steel frame, as seen here, like her successors built from 1927 to

1934. She survived in service till 1952, when she was sold to the Admiralty and stripped of her engines for experiments with underwater weapons at Portland. *J. Farley* was re-sold to private ownership in 1971, but languished unused on London River. This 1922 vessel of a 1906 design was the last surviving Mersey steam ferry, but by the time Merseyside decided to buy her back for preservation in 1985, she had been scrapped. *Commercial postcard*

Left **FRANCIS STOREY**, sister ship to *J. Farley*, was also built by Ailsa at Troon in 1922 (152 by 40 feet, 464 gross tons, 1,629 passengers) and named after a chairman of the Ferries Committee. She carried a canvas awning, often furled, on a timber frame over the promenade deck abaft the bridge and is pictured here in 1949 leaving Liverpool crowded with passengers for New Brighton. Like her sister ship, *Francis Storey* plied to Seacombe till 1927, then to Egremont and New Brighton, and was requisitioned for war service in 1942, fitting torpedo nets to merchant ships in Liverpool Bay. She was distinguished by a grey hull and buff funnel for sea and river cruises in 1934-36, and in post-war service by the Sampson post behind the funnel, inherited from wartime; this was a derrick and winch capable of lifting 5 tons, and when *Francis Storey* was laid up off the New Brighton service in winter she was used by Wallasey Corporation as a floating crane to replace gangways and stage rubbers in the annual repair and overhaul programme. When *Francis Storey* retired from service in 1951 she was sold to Cork Harbour Commissioners and renamed *Killarney* for use as a

tender to ocean liners and an excursion steamer. She was scrapped at Ballinacurra in 1960. *Still from a 9.5mm cine film by the late George Greenwood*

Above Built in 1932 as **ROYAL IRIS II** and renamed **ST HILARY** in 1950, this was the first Mersey ferry with three decks, the second, her sister ship *Royal Daffodil II*, following shortly in 1934. She was built by Harland & Wolff at Govan, 151 feet long, 48 feet in the beam and 697 gross tons, with engines by D. & W. Henderson of Glasgow. Her saloon, fitted out by Heaton, Tabbs of Liverpool, was panelled like a Tudor hall and furnished with upholstered leather seats with curved wooden armrests. This baronial domesticity was enhanced by a 6 feet by 4 feet painting of the former *Iris* and *Daffodil* in the Zeebrugge raid in 1918 (where is that picture now?). She was licensed to carry 2,024 passengers and is seen here as *Royal Iris II* approaching New Brighton Landing Stage. She dropped the suffix 'II' from her name in 1947 after the first *Royal Iris*, then working in Ireland, was renamed *Blarney*. This second *Royal Iris* was renamed *St Hilary* in 1950 after the patron saint of Wallasey, in preparation for the advent of the third *Royal Iris* in 1951. *St Hilary* was the name by which we knew this steamer in 1950-56, sailing from Seacombe and New Brighton to Liverpool and on cruises up the Manchester Ship Canal together with *Wallasey*. She left the Mersey in 1956 for Holland, where she was rebuilt as a diesel vehicular ferry for service between Dutch islands in the Rhine/Maas/Schelde delta. *Harvey Barton & Son postcard*

Below The 1950s ushered in the diesel era for Wallasey Ferries with the streamlined, diesel-electric **ROYAL IRIS**, the largest Mersey ferry ever built. She was designed to double as a cruise ship with a 60 feet by 40 feet dance hall, fish and chip saloon, buffet and bar. She was known locally as the 'booze boat' or the 'fish and chip boat'. Under the modern wrap was a standard three-deck Wallasey ferry, 150 feet by 48 feet, with massive timberwork in her decking and saloon doors. Her fish and chip saloon and smoke room were in a basement fourth deck next to the engine room and generators. Built in 1950-51 by William Denny & Brothers at Dumbarton, she had Ruston & Hornsby diesel engines driving generators to power Metropolitan Vickers electric propulsion motors, and was designed to damp noise and vibration from the engines. She had twice the volume of enclosed space of her steam predecessors, registering 1,234 gross tons. Her passenger capacity was 2,296 on ferry service or 1,000 on cruises as far as The Bar lightship and Manchester. She was painted custard yellow and pale green and carried a large plaque of the Wallasey borough coat of arms on the bridge. She finished ferrying in 1963, but carried on cruising. She lost her Wallasey plaque when Merseyside Transport was formed to take over the Corporation ferries and buses in 1969 (where is it now?). *J. Salmon postcard, copyright The Salmon Picture Library*

Bottom *Royal Iris* leaves New Brighton Pier and powers away from the landing stage on a cold, grey, blustery September day in 1951, her first season, with Bootle docks in the background. The landing stage was on the end of the Ferry Pier, but the picture was taken from the head of the separate Promenade Pier alongside, both owned by Wallasey Corporation. The Emetty, four-storey, octagonal rotunda perched on iron legs high above the water was a restaurant, with the West Cheshire Sailing Club on the first floor and above. With the advent of *Royal Iris* in 1951, the landing stage was lengthened by 60 feet with a separate pontoon (nicknamed 'Kon Tiki') to accommodate a ferry and cruise ship together.

The 1960s saw a decline in the fortunes of the New Brighton Ferry. A storm in 1962 badly damaged the stage and the two bridges, one of which was lifted off the pier head and sank. The ferry berth silted up, and from 1965 the service had to be suspended at low spring tides, when the landing stage was sitting on the sand. The last ferry sailed in 1971, and the Ferry Pier and stage were removed in 1973, the Promenade Pier surviving till 1978. With the closure of the Ferry Pier and the decline in 'jive and booze cruises', *Royal Iris* was given a new image, being repainted white and blue in a 1971-72 refit with a plush dining room (and no chip saloon) for lunches at Liverpool Landing Stage and afternoon and evening cruises. In 1985 she sailed round Land's End to the Pool of London with an exhibition to publicise trade and tourism on Merseyside, a round trip of 1,500 miles. She had a £3 million refit in 1990, but sailed her last cruise in 1991 and was put up for sale. In 1993 she was sold in good running order, but languished in Cardiff unused and was last seen derelict at a disused wharf on the south bank of Woolwich Reach on London River, where she was known as 'the electric iron'. *J. Salmon postcard, copyright The Salmon Picture Library*

Opposite above The next two ferries, **LEASOWE** of 1951 and *Egremont* of 1952, although relatively conventional in nautical design, were a break from the tradition of big Wallasey ferries from Scottish yards. Built by Philip & Son at Dartmouth, they were small at 138 feet by 34 feet with a limit of 1,472 passengers. They were the smallest Wallasey ferries since *Snowdrop* and *Crocus* of 1884-1906 and were bought to replace the retiring *J. Farley* and *Francis*

Storey. This new generation of diesel ferries had squat funnels and white, steel bridges and deckhouses. They carried an enclosed shelter on the forward promenade deck, which enhanced their gross tonnage to 567, while the main saloon, to compensate for the narrower hull, covered the full width of the main deck. There was only one gangway gate in the bulwark on each side instead of the normal two. The Crossley diesel engines, with direct drive, caused noise and vibration unknown on the stealthy steamers, despite air intake silencers and acoustic insulation of the engines. On the credit side, *Leasowe* and *Egremont* were economic, clean, fast and easy to

handle, cutting the Seacombe passage from 7 minutes (by steamer) to 5 minutes, and the New Brighton run from 30 to 20 minutes. They had upholstered seats in the main saloon and a bar and cafeteria below deck for the New Brighton service and for cruising, as they also plied on cruises out to Liverpool Bay and up to Manchester, when their passenger limit was reduced to 700. *Leasowe* was sold in 1974 and made her own way to Greece, where she was rebuilt for ferry service in the Aegean islands. *Egremont* had her machinery and screws removed after leaking and flooding in dock, was towed to Salcombe in 1976 and adapted as a floating sailing club. *Tokim postcard*

Below **ROYAL DAFFODIL II** was the last tonnage built for the Wallasey Corporation fleet and reverted to tradition in being of the normal dimensions of her steam consorts dating from 1927 to 1934, and having two gangway gates in the bulwarks on each side. She was a three-decker resembling *Royal Iris II/St Hilary* (1932-56) and *Royal Daffodil II* (1934), which was in turn renamed *St Hilary* before the new motorship arrived. The new ship was, in fact, the last of the old broad-beamed heavyweights from Scottish shipyards. She was built by James Lamont at Port Glasgow in 1957-58, 149 feet by 46 feet, 609 gross tons and licensed to carry 1,950 passengers. The main deck had two wing saloons, the second deck carried a solid rail, a central saloon and a forward saloon, and the third deck became the promenade deck. There was also a bar and buffet below deck for the New Brighton service. She sported two Wallasey coat of arms plaques, one each side of her funnel, until the amalgamation of the Mersey ferry fleets in 1969. (One of these plaques is kept in St Hilary's Church, Wallasey.) She replaced *Marlowe* (1927-58) on the Seacombe service and also plied to New Brighton and on cruises on summer weekends. In 1964 she sailed to Llandudno to tender to the Swedish cruise liner *Kungsholm*. *Commercial postcard*

Above **ROYAL DAFFODIL II** leaves Seacombe for Liverpool on a murky day in 1964 as tugs prepare to lead an Ellerman Line cargo ship into Alfred Dock to berth in the West Float. In 1968 *Royal Daffodil II* was holed below the waterline in a collision with a barge in fog, hurriedly landed her passengers at Liverpool and re-crossed the river. She was tied to a lamp post on Seacombe Promenade and settled up to her main deck in the water while awaiting low tide for repairs on the beach. Wallasey Corporation often beached its ferries between Seacombe and Egremont for repair as it was quicker and cheaper than going into dry dock. Later that year she dropped the suffix 'II' from her name after the demise of the Eagle steamer *Royal Daffodil* on London, Margate and cross-Channel excursions. The General Steam Navigation Company had inherited the famous name from its subsidiary, the New Medway Steam Packet Company, buying the original *Royal Daffodil* in 1932. The new *Royal Daffodil* was underpowered for her size, and with all the solid sail area displayed here on her second deck she was also difficult to manage in a cross-wind when berthing. After only 19 years of service on the Mersey she was sold to Greece in 1977 and partly rebuilt to carry vehicles aft. She is believed to be still on ferry service out of Piraeus.

Below   The floating landing stage and tollhouse of **SEACOMBE STEAMBOAT STATION** are viewed from a departing ferry steamer in 1950, the tower clock having just chimed 10.45. Gulls dot the roof of the waiting shed on the stage, with its empty belfry and decorative neo-Tudor timber framing. The main fog bell hung under the eaves above the stagemen's hut beneath the belfry. This stage was built in 1925,

480 feet long and 80 feet wide, with two hinged passenger bridges and three steamer berths (one for the goods ferry). The tollhouse was rebuilt in 1930-33 with its 90-foot-tall clock tower and the Wallasey Corporation ferry office and workshop alongside (off left). The radar scanner on top of the clock tower was installed in 1947 to guide both Wallasey and Birkenhead ferries across the busy shipping lanes in the smoky fogs ('smogs') of the coal age. Behind the ferry buildings we see Seacombe Ferry Hotel and streets of small terraced houses running down to the river. The waiting shed in this picture was replaced in 1973 and again, with a new stage, in 2000. Seacombe Ferry office today is the headquarters of Mersey Ferries. *The late George Greenwood*

Above right As the ferry drifts into the stage against the ebb tide we have this view of the north end of **SEACOMBE FERRY LANDING STAGE** in 1954, with its mooring chains, stage furniture and timber-framed, weatherboarded waiting shed, painted green and cream. The red lamp and two white lamps are stage marker lights, and the auxiliary fog bell next to the lamp post could be rung by a stagehand when ferries were landing on an ebb tide in a thick fog. (There were similar lights and a bell at the south end of the stage for ferries landing on the flood tide.) The river rushes by to seaward, leaving its tidemark on the red sandstone wall of the 1878-80 land reclamation for the ferry approach, incorporated into Seacombe Promenade when it was built in 1901.

A brewer's dray unloads barrels into the vaults of the four-storey Seacombe Ferry Hotel, which describes a graceful curve from Seacombe Promenade (right) into Victoria Place (left)

and leads the eye to the spire of St Paul's Parish Church (1846-91). The hotel was built in 1880-81 on completion of the land reclamation. Certain actors appearing at Liverpool theatres preferred to take the ferry to Seacombe to stay at this hotel because of its reputation for good cooking; it was the only hotel in Wallasey mentioned in *The Good Food Guide*. It closed in 1970.

Right In the 1950s the splendid tollhouse at Seacombe was something of a ferries museum with a display of seven model ferry steamers in glass cases depicting the development of Wallasey ferries over 125 years, from **SIR JOHN MOORE** (seen here) of 1826 to the streamlined *Royal Iris* of 1951, coincidentally both from the same shipyard. These models were on permanent display in the tollhouse, and are now in the Earlston Reference Library in Upper Brighton.

Sir John Moore was built in 1826 by Lang & Denny at Dumbarton for Jonathan Hulls of Kingstown (Dun Laoghaire) and named after an army officer from Glasgow who lived from 1701 to 1800. She was a wooden paddle-steamer only 104 feet long, 16ft 7in in the beam and 92 gross tons, but served as a mail steamer between Dun Laoghaire and the Clyde for seven years. In 1834 she was bought by James Atherton, the founder of New Brighton, to start the Liverpool-New Brighton Ferry service. This was the sole steamer on the service from 1834 till 1840, when she was joined by the iron paddle-steamer *Elizabeth*. The

PS *Queen of Beauty*, a second-hand luxury steam yacht, was added to the New Brighton Ferry fleet in 1845 for the exclusive use of the 1st Class clientele of Atherton's hillside villas, to segregate them from the new wave of Liverpool day-trippers to New Brighton sands. *Sir John Moore* was typical of the long-funnelled, open-decked paddle-steamers of the 1820s, '30s and '40s with a railed, open bridge spanning the paddle boxes and no shelter except a small saloon below deck next to the engine room. The tall funnel was guyed up with chains and she carried an auxiliary sail rig in case of engine failure. *Sir John Moore* retired from service in 1846 and became a houseboat moored on Tranmere shore. The model, built by Captain Kennedy in 1933, was photographed in 1964.

BIBLIOGRAPHY

The following is a list of publications from which I have gleaned and sifted information. All but Gore's and Kelly's Directories are in my own library at home.

A.B.C. of Motorcar Spotting (1949) by Graeme L. Greenwood

Annals of Birkenhead Ferries (lent to me by R. S. Cowan, general manager, in 1952)

An Atlas of Anglo-Saxon England (1981) by David Hill

Birkenhead: An Illustrated History (2003) by Ralph T. Brocklebank

Birkenhead Buses (1978) by Tom Turner

Birkenhead Corporation Transport Fare Lists and Timetables (1953)

Birkenhead Docks and Railways (1997) by Ken McCarron and David Marks

Birkenhead Guide (13 June 1969), a *Birkenhead News* supplement

Birkenhead Official Guide (1951)

Birkenhead of Yesterday (1985) by Carol E. Bidston

Birkenhead Priory and After (1950) by W. F. Bushell

The Birkenhead Railway (2000) by T. B. Maund

Birkenhead Yesterday and Today (1948) by W. R. S. McIntyre

British Labour Statistics Historical Abstract, 1886 to 1968 (1971) by the Department of Employment

British Railways Passenger Services (Midland Region, 1950)

British Railways Passenger Services (Western Region, 1952)

Cheshire ('The Buildings of England' series, 1971) by Nikolaus Pevsner and Edward Hubbard

Cheshire ('The King's England' series, 1938) by Arthur Mee

Crosville Official Time Table, Liverpool and Wirral districts (1949-50)

The Fall and Rise of Birkenhead Docks (1997) by Ken McCarron

First Street Railway Banquet in the Old World (1860) by Lee and Nightingale (facsimile reprint)

Gazetteer of the British Isles (1904) by J. G. Bartholomew

Golden Age of Buses (1978) by Charles F. Klapper

The Great Western North of Wolverhampton (1986) by Keith M. Beck

Gore's Directory and View of Liverpool and Environs (1832 et seq)

The History of Wallasey's Famous Ferry Services (1949) by Captain J. L. Regan

Kelly's Directory of Liverpool, Including Bootle, Birkenhead, Wallasey and Environs (1950s and '60s)

The Line Beneath the Liners: Mersey Railway Sights and Sounds (1983) by John W. Gahan

Local Transport in Birkenhead (1959) by T. B. Maund

The Mersey, Ancient & Modern (1878) by Benjamin Blower

The Mersey Estuary (1949) by J. E. Allison

Mersey Ferries, Volume 1 (Woodside to Eastham) (1991) by T. B. Maund
  Volume 2 (The Wallasey Ferries) (2003) by T. B. Maund and Martin Jenkins

Mersey Railway Electric Stock (1968) by J. E. Cull and B. J. Prigmore

Merseyside and District Railway Stations (1994) by Paul Bolger

The Mersey Tunnel (c1952) by the Mersey Tunnel Joint Committee

The Mighty Mersey and its Ferries (1992) by Richard Danielson

The Observer's Book of Ships (1952) by Frank E. Dodman

Old Ordnance Survey Maps by Alan Godfrey

A Postcard from the Fifties (2002) by Gillian Jackson

Popular Cars Illustrated (1949) by the Raleigh Press

Rails to Port and Starboard (Mersey dockside railways) (1992) by John W. Gahan

Railway Motor Buses and Bus Services in The British Isles, 1902-1933, Volume Two (1980) by John Cummings

Railway Stations of Wirral by the Merseyside Railway History Group

The Railway Heritage of Britain (1983) by Gordon Biddle and O. S. Nock

Reflections on a River (1995) by Paul Boot and Nigel Bowker

The Romance of Wirral (1949) by Alice Caton

Ships of the Mersey and Manchester (1959) by H. M. Le Fleming

Ships of the Seven Seas, Nos 1 and 2 (1947 and 1948) by Charles Graham

Sunlighters: The Story of a Village (1988) by Sue Sellers

The Survey Gazetteer of the British Isles (1951) by John Bartholomew

Thomas Brassey: Railway Builder (1969) by Charles Walker

The Tramways of Birkenhead and Wallasey (1987) by T. B. Maund and Martin Jenkins

West Coast Steamers (1956) by Christian Duckworth and Graham Langmuir

The Wirral Peninsula (1955) by Norman Ellison

Yesterday's Wirral Pictorial History, 1890 to 1953 (2000) by Ian and Marylin Boumphrey

INDEX